The
Year
of the
Poet VI

April 2019

The Poetry Posse

inner child press, ltd.

The Poetry Posse 2019

Gail Weston Shazor

Shareef Abdur Rasheed

Teresa E. Gallion

hülya n. yılmaz

Kimberly Burnham

Tzemin Ition Tsai

Elizabeth Esguerra Castillo

Jackie Davis Allen

Joe Paire

Caroline 'Ceri' Nazareno

Ashok K. Bhargava

Alicja Maria Kuberska

Swapna Behera

Albert 'Infinite' Carrasco

Eliza Segiet

William S. Peters, Sr.

General Information

The Year of the Poet VI
April 2019 Edition

The Poetry Posse

1st Edition : 2019

Publisher Information
1st Edition : Inner Child Press
intouch@innerchildpress.com
www.innerchildpress.com

ISBN-13 : 978-1-970020-79-3 (inner child press, ltd.)

$ 12.99

WHAT WOULD LIFE BE WITHOUT A LITTLE POETRY?

$\mathcal{D}$edication

This Book is dedicated to

Poetry . . .

The Poetry Posse

past, present & future

our Patrons and Readers

the Spirit of our Everlasting Muse

&

the Power of the Pen

to effectuate change!

In the darkness of my life
I heard the music
I danced...
and the Light appeared
and I dance

Janet P. Caldwell

Table of Contents

The Poetry Posse

Table of Contents . . . *continued*

April Featured Poets 115

$\mathcal{F}$oreword

West and Central Africa

I wish to look at West Africa and Central Africa from the socioeconomic and political aspect.

West and Central Africa are vast regions . The countries within these two regions were majorly colonised by the French. So, for this reason French language is commonly used among the people of these region in addition to English and the various native languages. Most people from these two regions have very strong ties with the French.

Politically West and Central Africa regions have experienced political turmoil for many years. There has been instability in these two regions of Africa. Various governments within these two regions have had challenges as far as democracy and human rights are concerned. A lot needs to be done to strengthen democracy and respect for human rights within these two regions. Cases of political rebellion are rampant here. There is also increase in violations of human rights. These are regions where child soldiers are found and terrible violations of women rights.

The economic situation in West and Central Africa is no better. Due to political instability in these two regions, the economy here has also worsened.

High inflation rate, unemployment among young people and poor infrastructural development can be observed in these regions. A lot must be done to help change the situation in these regions.

Hillary Mainga

Director

The Hillary Mainga Foundation

Busia County, Kenya

~ * ~

The Hillary Mainga Foundation was established in 2005 with the main objective of supporting education of needy children in Kenya and for socioeconomic support of women, youths and the poor elderly persons. This foundation has since helped many children's acquire their education and a number of women and youths have been economically supported through their community groups. However the foundation has had its own challenges majorly in funding its activities as it purely depends on individual well wishers whose donations cannot support many activities as its unreliable. Also the number of needy children who actually require educational support is very high and the foundation lack resources to support all those needy children. This foundation therefore appeals to well wishers ,groups and organizations to come forward for partnership with a view of helping it to achieve its objectives of supporting education of needy children and communities socioeconomically.

Comntact information :

hillarymaingafoundation@yahoo.com

Poets, Writers . . . know that we are the enchanting magicians that nourishes the seeds of dreams and thoughts . . . it is our words that entice the hearts and minds of others to believe there is something grand about the possibilities that life has to offer and our words tease it forth into action . . . for you are the Poet, the Writer to whom the Gift of Words has been entrusted . . .

~ wsp

Preface

Dear Family and Friends,

Yes I am excited? This year we have aligned our vision with that of UNESCO as it honors and acknowledges a variety of Global Indigenous cultures. We are now in our sixth year of publication. As are on our way to hitting another milestone. Needless to say, I am elated. Our initial vision was to just perform at this level for the year of 2014. Since that time we have had the blessed opportunity to include many other wonderful word artists and storytellers in the Poetry Posse from lands, cultures and persuasions all over the world. We have featured hundreds of additional poets, thereby introducing their poetic offerings to our vast global readership.

In keeping with our effort and vision to expand the awareness of poets from all walks by making this offerings accessible, we at Inner Child Press International will continue to make every volume a FREE Download. The books are also available for purchase at the affordable cost of $7.00 per volume.

In the previous years, our monthly themes were Flowers, Birds, Gemstones, Trees and Past

Cultures. This year we have elected to continue the Cultural theme. In each month's volume you will have the opportunity to not only read at least one poem themed by our Poetry Posse members about such culture, but we have included a few words about the culture in our prologue. The reasoning behind this is that now our poetry has the opportunity to be educational for not only the reader, but we poets as well. We hope you find the poetic offerings insightful as we use our poetic form to relay to you what we too have learned through our research in making our offering available to you, our readership.

In closing, we would like to thank you for being an integral part of our amazing journey.

Enjoy our amazing featured poets . . . they are amazing!

Building Cultural Bridges of Understanding . . .

Bless Up . . . From the home in our hearts to yours

Bill

The Poetry Posse
Inner Child Press Ineternational

PS

Do Not forget about the World Healing, World Peace Poetry effort.

Available here

www.worldhealingworldpeacepoetry.com

**For Free Downloads of Previous Issues of
The Year of the Poet**

www.innerchildpress.com/the-year-of-the-poet

poetry is . . .

Central and West Africa

Central and West Africa has a history that predates that of the European continent coming of age. Since then, Africa, and specifically Centran and West Africa has ehe onslaght of Misionaries, Colonizers, Slave Traders and Resource Theievs. These invaders were primarily made up of the Dutch, English, French, Spanish, and whomever else that saw these regions of Africa as a opportunity to enrich themselves and their regimes. Much of the art and other cultural items were plundered and transported back to their native countries. One of the largest holocaust' occurred in the Congo and surrounding region at the hands of many despots to include King Leopold, Cecil B. Rhodes, Napolean and many more. The Germans invaded and colonized various regions which are now know as Cameroon, Tanzania, Uganda, and Namibia. Their reach also extended beyond the west to the Pacific ocean thereby

givining cause to and leaving uncountable casualties and
suffering in their wake.

West Africa

Poets . . .
sowing seeds in the
Conscious Garden of Life,
that those who have yet to come
may enjoy the Flowers.

I Fly

because I Can

...said the Dreamer to the world.

www.iamjustbill.com

The
Year
of the
Poet VI

April 2019

The Poetry Posse

Poetry succeeds where instruction fails.

~ wsp

Gail Weston Shazor

Gail Weston Shazor

This is a creative promise ~ my pen will speak to and for the world. Enamored with letters and respectful of their power, I have been writing for most of my life. A mother, daughter, sister and grandmother I give what I have been given, greatfilledly.

Author of . . .

"An Overstanding of an Imperfect Love"
&
Notes from the Blue Roof

Lies My Grandfathers Told Me

available at Inner Child Press.

www.facebook.com/gailwestonshazor
www.innerchildpress.com/gail-weston-shazor
navypoet1@gmail.com

Thunder and Lightening

Where just a sliver of light
Finds its way into loam
The depression created
By thunder bounces
Against the sky erratically
And I reach for your hand
Winding my breath around
The forefinger and thumb
Because I want my heart held
We talk of sex
With the honesty of expectations
That occur naturally and with a
Spontaneity in a lifetime
Of familiarity
Time has no hold on this
Our kinetic friendship
Because I knew you
Long before I was meant
For you to find in places unlooked
It is here in the darkest moments
With your back against
The sturdy spine of trees
I can fit inside the palms
That rest against the bent hip
Of my softness, gentleness
The coaxing of calmness
Against the temperance of a quickening
And I am no longer alone
Within this lightening storm
I keep hidden those words
Said in haste but always
Measured against the moment

Of someone else's parting
Of our enclosed solitude
The pain of which has faded
In learning what is important about
My heart locked into the space
Between thumb and forefinger
And yours ever in my soul

A Senryu a Haiku, a Nonet, a Couplet and a dream

Greying dreams transmute
Old memories into dust
Across still water

Drums always will beat
Requiring attention
Of a calling sound

The
Movement
Make cadence
Of the sounds
Gathered on the wind
The breath of whispering
And the black soil of the earth
The offering of new rainfalls
Until it is now in completion

I threw the jagged edges of the broken pieces
Into the rising sun

Two Continents

I weave you into my net
Each knot a reminder
Of why you are here
In the creases of my fingers
The dust that travels
From my Sahara to yours
 Tightens the bond
Of remembrances
And I smile at the cuts
Across the pads of my thumbs
And I wish for the rains

And I wish for the rains
To carry this bottle
Containing all my love
From this shore to that one
You, verdant and lush
Me, arid and dry
Until we both get to the ocean
Where my thirst is slacked
And your flow stemmed
There the flowers grow
In the joining

Gail Weston Shazor

Alicja Maria Kuberska

Alicja Maria Kuberska – awarded Polish poetess, novelist, journalist, editor. She was born in 1960, in Świebodzin, Poland. She now lives in Inowrocław, Poland.
In 2011 she published her first volume of poems entitled: "The Glass Reality". Her second volume "Analysis of Feelings", was published in 2012. The third collection "Moments" was published in English in 2014, both in Poland and in the USA. In 2014, she also published the novel - "Virtual roses" and volume of poems "On the border of dream". Next year her volume entitled "Girl in the Mirror" was published in the UK and "Love me" , " (Not)my poem" in the USA. In 2015 she also edited anthology entitled "The Other Side of the Screen".

In 2016 she edited two volumes: "Taste of Love" (USA), "Thief of Dreams" (Poland) and international anthology entitled " Love is like Air" (USA). In 2017 she published volume entitled "View from the window" (Poland). She also edits series of anthologies entitled "Metaphor of Contemporary" (Poland)

Her poems have been published in numerous anthologies and magazines in Poland, the USA, the UK, Albania, Belgium, Chile, Spain, Israel, Canada, India, Italy, Uzbekistan, Czech Republic, South Korea and Australia. She was a featured poet of New Mirage Journal (USA) in the summer of 2011.

Alicja Kuberska is a member of the Polish Writers Associations in Warsaw, Poland and IWA Bogdani, Albania. She is also a member of directors' board of Soflay Literature Foundation.

Nigeria

Where are the speakers proclaiming fiery words of
indignation?
Where are politicians issuing moving condolences?
Where are the journalists howling genocide?
Where are priests of all religions praying for the dead?
Where are you humans?
Where?
The contemporary world resembles a cup
Filled itself to the brim
Hypocrisy, duplicity and mendacity,
I accuse you of the sin of mute indifference.
Nigeria is crying with tears of blood.
Soaking in the mass graves
Of her children.

It is she

We pass each other nearly every day,
Distance of fear between us.
Life forces us to mutual disregard and acceptance.
At times, like an unruly child, she will spoil something,
To garner attention, to arrest with a gesture.

I see her in the wind, which carelessly
Turns over the withering leaves
And standing proudly erect in stalks stiffened by frost.
She paints shriveled trees gray, breaks limbs with a crack.
She is mute in the clenched throats of birds,
She stares with glassy eyes.

She is all-around and she reminds us of her presence.
She patiently explains the meaning of certainty.
I know she does not allow us to take anything,
When she plays the requiem and invites eternal sleep

Autumn love

You kissed me.
I felt a bittersweet taste in my mouth.
I closed my eyes.
In my imagination I saw the park.
Do you remember?
You said we were like two trees in autumn.

Look,
naive, youthful thoughts flew off
 -frivolous, migratory birds.
The first chill chased them.
Their joyous trill,
glorifying a perfect love, rang out.
Delusions fell to the ground like leaves,
rotting and turning to dust.
We are firmly rooted in the soil of everyday life.

Jackie

Davis

Allen

Jackie Davis Allen, otherwise known as Jacqueline D. Allen or Jackie Allen, grew up in the Cumberland Mountains of Appalachia. As the next eldest daughter of a coal miner father and a stay at home mother, she was the first in her family to attend and graduate from college. Her siblings, in their own right, are accomplished, though she is the only one, to date, that has discovered the gift of writing.

Graduating from Radford University, with a Bachelors of Science degree in Early Education, she taught in both public and private schools. For over a decade she taught private art classes to children both in her home and at a local Art and Framing Shop where she also sold her original soft sculptured Victorian dolls and original christening gowns.

She resides in northern Virginia with her husband, taking much needed get-aways to their mountain home near the Blue Ridge Mountains, a place that evokes memories of days spent growing up in the Appalachian Mountains.

A lover of hats, she has worn many. Following marriage to her college sweetheart, and as wife, mother, grandmother, teacher, tutor, artist, writer, poet and crafter, she is a lover of art and antiques, surrounding herself, always, with books, seeking to learn more.

In 2015 she authored *Looking for Rainbows, Poetry, Prose and Art*, and in 2017, *Dark Side of the Moon*. Both books of mostly narrative poetry were published by Inner Child Press and were edited by hulya n. yilmaz.

http://www.innerchildpress.com/jackie-davis-allen.php
jackiedavisallen.com

African Trees

I am me,
More than your eyes can see.
In shades of black, brown,
Chocolate, mocha and everything
In between. I'm a God given-gift!

I may have even descended
From a King! Or a Queen!

Maybe, perchance
If you would but open your eyes,
You'd be surprised
To find my skin color is found
All around the world.

That my roots reach all the way back
To the continent of Africa.

My unknown ancestors
Hid from soul-less monsters.
Yet, like animals they were tossed
Into the stinking belly of a ship.
Beaten, starved, many died.

All enslaved, sailing far away from home.
From Africa. Eventually, sold at the market.

DNA say's I've family ties
Both in Central and Western Africa.
One day, God willing,
I'll go back there, see for my self.
But, have you heard of Henry Gates?

With the tools of technology,
He's discovering African Trees!

Heart of the Poet

There is no question
That the seasons are changing.
And that time still marches on,
Regardless of whether or not
I use my gifts and talent.

Yet, can you comprehend how amazing
It was for me to discover my dusty, dormant gifts,
Lying unopened behind the prideful door?

And can you imagine
How surprised I was
To discover the key.
To unlocking them, was to use them
More and more?

Today, O Lord, humbly and gratefully I celebrate!
For it is in the investment of my creativity
That they have been multiplied!

It all seems quite amazing
That I am living with no regrets!
For it is in the tasting and savoring of my gifts
That the newest portrait
Of my life is being painted.

O Lord, I humbly and gratefully thank you:
My days are filled with purpose and passion.
May others find the key that unlocks their identity!

What is Joy?

Come with me
And we will hike through the mountains.
And escaping into our daydreams,
We will pluck wildflowers for our hair!
We will leap over boulders and peek
Into days gone by.

Do you remember when we were young?
We roamed through the ancient mountains
Where caves and waterfalls fueled our
Childhood dreams and fantasies
Of days soon to be long gone by,
One of us losing a shoe.

Do you remember a day in the mountains,
The two of us, hands clutching thickened vines,
Our entwined legs wrapped around? And how
We attempted to make those Tarzan yells?
And how the vine broke and the two of us
Tumbled down the side of the mountain?

Let us relive these childhood moments
When we hiked through the mountains
And escaped into our daydreams.
With wildflowers tucked into our hair,
Let us leap, once again
Into unadulterated joy!

Tzemin Ition Tsai

Dr. Tzemin Ition Tsai (蔡澤民博士) was born in Republic of China, in 1957. He holds a Ph.D. in Chemical Engineering and two Masters of Science in Applied Mathematics and Chemical Engineering. He is a professor at Asia University (Taiwan), editor of "Reading, Writing and Teaching" academic text. He also writes the long-term columns for Chinese Language Monthly in Taiwan.

He is a scholar with a wide range of expertise, while maintaining a common and positive interest in science, engineering and literature member.

He has won many national literary awards. His literary works have been anthologized and published in books, journals, and newspapers in more than 40 countries and have been translated into more than a dozen languages.

That Pink Clouds Always Like to Follow Us

Sunset leads dusk. In the small alley
All turned into long oblique shadows
We get rely on so close
Do not try to eavesdrop on, the road with the pink clouds
Fireflies seem so mysterious under the shade
Bypassing the backyard, Magnoli higher than the wall
Aroma of the flowers hastily proclaim the advent of night
Our two-hand more tightly
Let the little yellow mud road, only suit to walk slowly

The memories still fresh laughs loudly and scared
Maniac informal bouncing and vivacious still in sight
Watching you, Awoke
This winding road, with over thirty years of effort
Day by day, Step by step
Was printed on yellow mud, how many pebbles
Near the thin soil, Oxalis flower still sneaking around
What happened?
When your hair black and white mixed but so clear?
Gently stroking, hanging forehead hair
Both distressed and pleased
Fortunately, your eyebrows did not follow into white

Small ditches less than half a foot
At the bottom of the path
Missed my footing, how you get giggled so mischievous
Just Like you were in youth
Implying, Pink clouds deliberately teasing the memory box
In the past, Maniac uninhibited dance
Now you and I both need a hand gently hold

Return on, The Magnolia also sneaking around waiting
Silence like a fairy
Pick them off one, hanging on your hair
You finally shy in silence
But more than this floral scent
To be able to stop the night
To take you away from quietly
Please moon to illuminate the path home
But
I can't find the slightest drowsiness

Yellow Butterflies visit Michelia

Into the front of the yellow dirt road
Vaguely, appear a corner of the old home
Under the red cream tile
When the old man' figure in our family less one again
In a spirit of fear back home
With joy and miss
Playing barefoot, yellow soil is so sticky
Mother's call even in the ears with the slightest
reverberation
Like the dream before wake up

Butterflies still visit the Michelia in our courtyard
Blankly memories, that year the Michelia celebrate with
bearing a red fruit for my for my birth
The only one red fruit
Mother always said that's my baby
I could not help but giggle and giggle laugh
Until today, finally know that the original sinking fruit
actually is my mother
Michelia no longer bears fruits
Just like
That yellow butterflies are still visiting the Michelia
Always silently, Facing at each other with me

Window

Should be said so
Voyeuristic desires
Strongly occupied my mind from childhood
Maybe I am a born bad Cotyledons
Always know how to
One step ahead
Board the newly built wall
And then never leave

Gradually dark each day
That little lonely lamp full house yellow
At the moment, be moved by that scene of mother feeds
baby
Suddenly, Respect for the novice father cover the baby with
a quilt
Did not notice, the sun and the moon turns hurried
footsteps outside
When my little master learned
Secretly riding on my shoulder to respond
The call of childhood from the downstairs

In fact, always more than just
Even obediently close the curtains
Spring love to set off a corner at midnight
Prick up ears
Eavesdropping the love songs lingering all night

Tzemin Ition Tsai

Shareef
Abdur
Rasheed

Shareef Abdur Rasheed

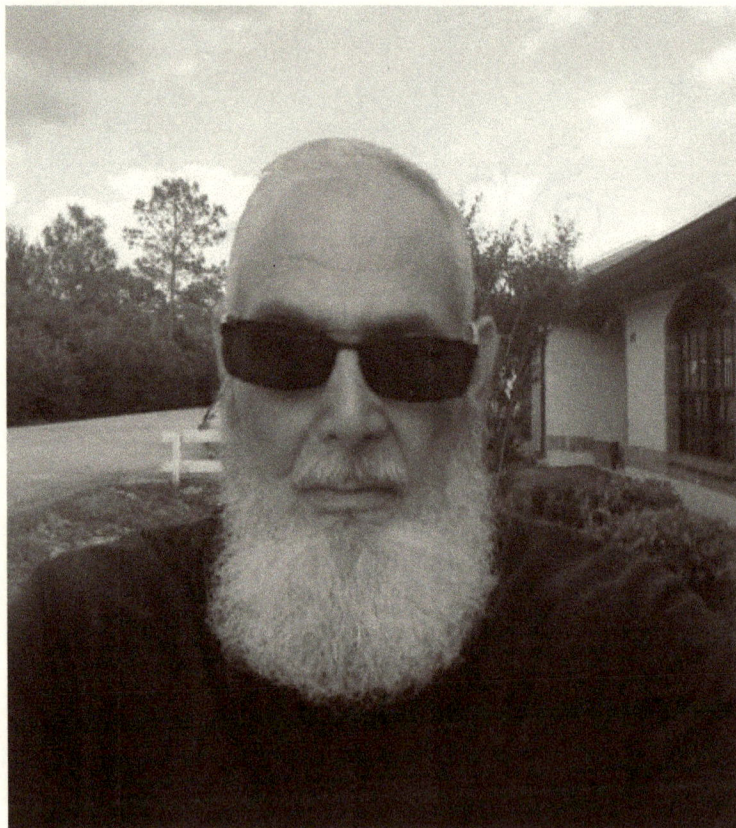

Shareef Abdur-Rasheed, AKA Zakir Flo was born and raised in Brooklyn, New York. His education includes Brooklyn College, Suffolk County Community College and Makkah, Saudi Arabia. He is a Veteran of the Viet Nam era, where in 1969 he reverted to his now reverently embraced Islamic Faith. He is very active in the Islamic community and beyond with his teachings, activism and his humanity.

Shareef's spiritual expression comes through the persona of "Zakir Flo" . Zakir is Arabic for "To remind". Never silent, Shareef Abdur-Rasheed is always dropping science, love, consciousness and signs of the time in rhyme.

Shareef is the Patriarch of the Abdur-Rasheed Family with 9 Children (6 Sons and 3 Daughters) and 41 Grandchildren (24 Boys and 17 Girls).

For more information about Shareef, visit his personal FaceBook Page at :

https://www.facebook.com/shareef.abdurrasheed1
https://zakirflo.wordpress.com

Drum cries

lament
millions died
drum roll cries
" so many souls,
  so many died "
so many raped,
violate, subjugate,
humiliate,

drum cries

" dam you want me to
tell you?
you want to know about
motherland cradle of
all humanity
yet historically drenched
in humility
exploited constantly
you hear West Africa
you hear Slavery

drum cries

Mf'ers you hear me,
kidnapped me,
separated my people from me
till dem not know dem from me
stripped identity
stripped resources from my body
your Europeans armed,
harmed me

drum cries

" our blackness demonized
taken by surprise
packed in slave ships
many not to survive the trip
of those that did many wished
they too didn't arrive
greeted by the whip
dehumanized, bought, sold
a people they stole
drum tells story
not his-story
this land home of all humanity
enriched naturally
diamonds, gold,
silver, iron ore,
only scratch the surface
great civilizations, centers of
scientific knowledge
Mali empire, Mansa Musa
they performed eye surgery
while Europe languished in
poverty, relative obscurity,
irrelevantly
yet they came
English, Dutch, French,
Portuguese, Germans
raped me, uprooted my
family

drum cries

" You want a story, history
of what happened to me
a land of beauty, majesty,
birthplace of humanity? "

Shareef Abdur Rasheed

it would take many sunrises,
sunsets yet the story would
only begin
so much the history of
Africa and Africans "

listen to the drum

it still cries

food4thought = education

hitting..,

the path walked long before you were born
narrow filled complete with thistles, thorns
broken glass, body remains turned ashes
blood stains splashed on the narrow but
straight path
all signs point, righteous was here
carrying great weight to bare
kept eye on prize overcame fear
even though the prize often seemed far
hardly near
they knew the promise of Allah(swt)
is true
worth the wait what's waiting for you
faithful slaves who were willing and
gave the world away
for a better place that never goes
away
feared their lord and judgement day
to enjoy gardens beneath which
rivers flow
with milk and honey
time don't go
nobody grows old
unlike the plight of the crooked path
looks good wide and smooth
says " come on we got something for you
to adore, it will adore you,
you'll keep wanting more
it keeps wanting you"
sounds profound, too good to be true
that's why this path is made to look,
sound to accommodate you
hem you in sin hypnotize, misguide

the glitter takes you by surprise
blinds spiritual eyes
on this path seemingly a smooth ride
is deception, element of surprise
waiting to lay waste to misguide
mankind who hurried in haste
left the prize behind, lost the race
never to taste heavenly wine,
silk pillows recline, dine with those
who wisely took the path free
of wrath
divine bliss bestowed on those
who chose and pursued this ultimate,
eternal, merciful gift
and ultimately enjoy the last laugh
that comes with it.

food4thought = education

as flowers..,

wither, leaves fall,
birds make their winter
sojourn seeking relief
everything's brief
things we seek
words we speak
thoughts we think
as is youth dem flee
truth remains steady
illusion brings plenty
false conclusions
especially if it leads
to delusions because
humans don't like reality
though true words can
survive to stay alive
in hearts and minds
as those put to pen
may collect dust can
but once again
thrust into relevance
when situations emerge
life has a way with words
impact retention
fact of the matter is,
life's reality has a way of
getting one's attention
yo..word!

food4thought = education

Shareef Abdur Rasheed

Kimberly Burnham

Find yourself in the pattern. As a 28-year-old photographer, Kimberly Burnham appreciated beauty. Then an ophthalmologist diagnosed her with a genetic eye condition saying, "Consider life, if you become blind." She discovered a healing path with insight, magnificence, and vision. Today, 33 years later, a poet and neurosciences expert with a PhD in Integrative Medicine, Kimberly's life mission is to change the global face of brain health. Using health coaching, Reiki, Matrix Energetics, craniosacral therapy, acupressure, and energy medicine, she supports people in their healing from brain, nervous system, and chronic pain issues. As managing editor of Inner Child Magazine, Kimberly's 2019 project is peace, language, and visionary poetry with her recently published book, *Awakenings: Peace Dictionary, Language and the Mind, a Daily Brain Health Program.*

http://www.NerveWhisperer.Solutions
https://www.linkedin.com/in/kimberlyburnham

Yorùbá Concept of Peace

Language evolves
the Yorùbá word for peace is "àlàáfíà"
all is well in all aspects of life
peace at both individual and social levels
with a handful of "ìrépọ̀" harmony
and a dollop of "ìsọ̀kan" unity
components all of "àlàáfíà ìlú"
peace in society

Language evolves
"àlàáfíà" some say borrowed from the Hausa "lafiya"
good health borrowed from Arabic
"afiyah" health while other words continue to explore
a way of thinking and being
"örê" peace and calm
"itelorun" contentment
"ifokanbale" lack of worry
"sùúrù" peace and patience

Languages evolves
some focused more on wellbeing and balance
others health and peace
seeing the individual
an integral part of the cosmic forces
elements and nature balanced "àlàáfíà"
and with "zaman lafiya" in Hausa
comes a sense of inner peace

Peace Baskets

In a bright blue and white dress
with dark and light shades of blue
she smiles out at me through the camera
across the miles
behinds her a mountain of baskets
intense red and white
black with green juxtaposed
and I wonder at her smile
the text next to her picture tells me
she from the Huye district of Rwanda
a survivor of genocide
a member of the "Agaseke k'Amahoro" Cooperative
"amahoro" the peace she works toward
with split bamboo and raffia
the leaves of a palm tree
native to tropical Africa and Madagascar
she creates one basket at a time
broken lines of black wind round and round
through the white woven strands
of "Agaseke k'Amahoro" peace baskets
that hold flowers, clothing and blankets
side by side with hopes and dreams
of "amahoro"

An Ancient Peace

In the Oldupai Gorge
seat of an ancient civilization
the Maasai of Kenya and Tanzania
say "eseriani" not only for peace
but togetherness
communication, health and ultimately the peace of mind
that characterize this birthplace of humans
this "place of peace"
"eseriani"

Elizabeth E. Castillo

Elizabeth Esguerra Castillo is a multi-awarded and an Internationally-Published Contemporary Author/Poet and a Professional Writer / Creative Writer / Feature Writer / Journalist / Travel Writer from the Philippines. She has 2 published books, "Seasons of Emotions" (UK) and "Inner Reflections of the Muse", (USA). Elizabeth is also a co-author to more than 60 international anthologies in the USA, Canada, UK, Romania, India. She is a Contributing Editor of Inner Child Magazine, USA and an Advisory Board Member of Reflection Magazine, an international literary magazine. She is a member of the American Authors Association (AAA) and PEN International.

Web links:

Facebook Fan Page

https://free.facebook.com/ElizabethEsguerraCastillo

Google Plus

https://plus.google.com/u/0/+ElizabethCastillo

Nomads of Sahel

Blessed are you -
With your rugged terrain
Nestled in the Sahara Desert,
In the long forgotten land of Mali.

In a brief sojourn, one can see-
The eclectic life of the Fulani,
"Blue men of the desert" they are called
Clothed in mystic, indigo robes and turbans.

Children of Sahel -
Born in a semi-arid steppe country,
Running on dry soil, famished
Victims of civil war, drought, and large-scale migration.

Indigo Child

I am not of this world -
i came from an abysmal chaos-
but from this beautiful chaos, Desiderata was born-
a child of the Universe, precious and golden
a lovely old soul beyond time and space-
often misunderstood by mediocre minds-
but applauded by great free thinkers -
i long for a world enveloped in serenity-
inhabited by empaths with great sensitivity
a loner I may be but this is who I am-
but i've got this deep connection with things around me
an indigo girl at birth-
my temporary sanctuary is the Earth
lonewolves gather at my feet-
for i am their Goddess in human form.

Cosmogonic Love

If your star and my star accidentally aligned in their
    intertwining paths,
It's not their fault that you and I suddenly collide
Collide in these cosmic hues of forbidden territory,
A million of eons away, we were two kindred souls who
    were destined to meet
In a world of oblivion where imperfection is dreaded,
Though we must love one another's imperfections to
    recognize it is really True Love...
Beyond time and space, beyond universes, beyond the limit
    of light years
You and I were destined to cross each other's galaxies
A billions constellations will guide you on your way to me
For the King and Queen of this Cosmogonic Love to finally
    meet.

Joe
Paire

Joe Paire

Joseph L Paire' aka Joe DaVerbal Minddancer . . .
is a quiet man, born in a time where civil liberties
were a walk on thin ice. He's been a victim of his
own shyness often sidelined in his own quest for
love. He became the observer, charting life's path.
Taking note of the why, people do what they do.
His writings oft times strike a cord with the
dormant strings of the reader. His pen the rosined
bow drawn across the mind. He comes full-frontal
or in the subtlest way, always expressing in a way
that stimulate the senses.

www.facebook.com/joe.minddancer

Are You Just Another Land Motherland

will I know you from memory motherland?
My early drawings are reminiscent of yours
Sidewalks and brick walls tell of me
Carved stones and empty tombs tell of you

Am I missing from your history?
I'm center stage to your misery
Can I go to a place not known as home?
Can I feel a sense of security?
Who are you Africa?

Center of the world center of debate
Topical tropical deserted and abandoned
Expected to go back land
Is this all the resources you got man?
There is a beauty to you Africa

Dark blues follow fallen skies
And there's a star to the east
Is your land under my feet?
The bridge of my nose seemed posed
Like stones to braided chin
Pyramids of life from the death of men

Statues here tell me a different tale
Can I get away from my mental state?
Can I truly be free of hate if I go there?
Africa
Are you just another land motherland?

House Tiger

She flicks her tail and lies in wait
Honey mustard yellow and cream
The Serengeti connection is clear in her chi
Sage and high energy ground rosehips
She nudges my hand away purring

Purring a yawn with beautiful fangs
Stretching out her claws to swipe a treat
Fuzzy little teardrop lay by my side to sleep
I dare not move as I lay like prey

Feeding time has no schedule
She plays when she wants you
A gaze like who are you?
Finicky little she is my pet

Desert sand in a litter box
Jungle trees in my closet
Leaping creeping as she fast attacks
It seems a plastic bag entered her terrain

Exploratory creature in nature of square footage
Let me brush my hoodie free
my furniture burnisher and turn pieces
My inhouse beasty
Sucking trough my teeth speech and she comes

She made the case to try slides
My shoe laces have bye
Nocturnal eyes glow in darkness
Her legion roves through darkness
House Tiger purrs

Ocean To Ocean

My east is your west Africa
Atlantic waters of common souls
I can't speak of known treasures
Your butterflies cause my weather
And the beaches erode on both plains
We were joined at the hip long ago
city country city and we split
Rejoined by sailing ships
West of my east and we can't sleep
So many babies born in poverty
I see your flies do you see my casualties
Ocean to ocean come and talk to me
I'll walk on vacation sands and white beaches
Taste the fruit fresh plucked from greed
I'd love to talk a little bit more
About your riches and history
Your culture your diversity
Climate change aside they tell me you're hot
While I slumber in the summer of shared dreams
Ocean to ocean follow me east

hülya
n.
yılmaz

hülya n. yılmaz

A retired Liberal Arts professor, hülya n. yılmaz [sic] is Co-Chair and Director of Editing Services at Inner Child Press International, and a literary translator. Her poetry has been published in an excess of sixty anthologies of global endeavors. Two of her poems are permanently installed in *TelePoem Booth*, a nation-wide public art exhibition in the U.S. She has shared her work in Kosovo, Canada, Jordan and Tunisia. hülya has been honored with a 2018 WIN Award of British Colombia, Canada. She is presently working on three poetry books and a short-story collection. hülya finds it vital for everyone to understand a deeper sense of self and writes creatively to attain a comprehensive awareness for and development of our humanity.

hülya n. yılmaz, Ph.D.

Writing Web Site
hulyanyilmaz.com

Editing Web Site
hulyasfreelancing.com

The Igbu Landing

Denial came as it still tends to do.
"It's only a legend", shouted the well-to-do.
In his time or now, he was no legend however,
Roswell King, the white overseer.
His ink had mastered a horrifying account;
Not far away, but from a plantation nearby.
Pierce Butler was the name of the God-forsaken place
Where the white overseer once again put history to shame.
Those died in mass suicide were given not one single name.

Dunbar Creek

It is etched in history's fair ink,
So, let their freedom-speech be our link:
Their high chief led the fatal march.

The marshy waters of Dunbar Creek
May have never even imagined to seek
Such suffering, such pain, such a sacrifice.

Many drowned bodies were later found.
Though it fails us, an actual account
There is no reason for us to doubt . . .

75 Igbu slaves had committed themselves
To a mass suicide on that dark day in 1803.
Each of them only wanted to be free,
Nothing unlike you and me.

The Gullah Folklore

As a story of resistance, unlike many others
Comes to us the still-bleeding Igbu-slave-struggles.
They were held captive by the white men.
In sum, his bloody story was at it again!

Death over slavery, therein lies the Igbu-strength.
African folklore lends room to such courage at length.
White His-tory tried to put all valid accounts on trial.
Yet, post-1980-research laid out the facts with breadth.

The site of their passing onto their freedom through death
Has in September, 2002 finally been pronounced "holy".
It was the same St. Simons African American community
That asked attendees to honor their ancestors' eternal rest.

As a story of resistance, unlike many others
Comes to us the still-bleeding Igbu-slave-struggles.
They were held captive by the white men.
In sum, his bloody story was at it again!

Teresa
E.
Gallion

Teresa E. Gallion

Teresa E. Gallion was born in Shreveport, Louisiana and moved to Illinois at the age of 15. She completed her undergraduate training at the University of Illinois Chicago and received her master's degree in Psychology from Bowling Green State University in Ohio. She retired from New Mexico state government in 2012.

She moved to New Mexico in 1987. While writing sporadically for many years, in 1998 she started reading her work in the local Albuquerque poetry community. She has been a featured reader at local coffee houses, bookstores, art galleries, museums, libraries, Outpost Performance Space, the Route 66 Festival in 2001 and the State of Oklahoma's Poetry Festival in Cheyenne, Oklahoma in 2004. She occasionally hosts an open mic.

Teresa's work is published in numerous Journals and anthologies. She has two CDs: *On the Wings of the Wind* and *Poems from Chasing Light*. She has published three books: *Walking Sacred Ground, Contemplation in the High Desert* and *Chasing Light*.

Chasing Light was a finalist in the 2013 New Mexico/Arizona Book Awards.

The surreal high desert landscape and her personal spiritual journey influence the writing of this Albuquerque poet. When she is not writing, she is committed to hiking the enchanted landscapes of New Mexico. You may preview her work at

http://bit.ly/1aIVPNq or *http://bit.ly/13IMLGh*

Cameroon

The history of your geography and culture
tells us the diversity of your cultures, beliefs,
languages and lifestyles embrace stability and
conflict blended with affluence and poverty.
Your country has the nickname, Mini Africa.

Looking from the outside you appear resilient
in spite of wars and conflicts surrounding you
and upheavals within your own boundaries.
You survive under the pressure of horrific violence,
poverty, hunger, disease and sickness. One wonders
what karmic burdens you inherited to showcase you
as a small version of an entire Continent.

You still fight and kill each other in the 21st century.
It seems to be the nature of Africa to resolve
differences with violence just as all humans do
across planet earth. Will humanity ever come
to terms with the concept of living in harmony?

Bitter Memory

Hush hush bitter memory
clutching my sleeveless jacket.
Your salty tongue reaches

into the canyons of my body
balanced on the high wire of my heart.
Your saintly robes brush hard

against my skin. I want to
face the day without you.
Go back to your worm hole.

Wait until I am ready
to sit next to you
for my history lesson.

Continental Breakfast

Two boiled eggs, a bowl of cereal,
yoplait yogurt and a cup of coffee.
Breakfast on my private balcony.

The sweet melody of the river,
the best dessert on the planet
beats all the competition.

It is hard to focus on anything
except the sound and light
flowing in the river.

Reflecting on the moment
as the stomach swells
with food and gratitude.

At a loss for descriptive words
to capture this moment.
Notice the grin on my face.

Ashok
K.
Bhargava

Ashok Bhargava is a poet, writer, community activist, public speaker, management consultant and a keen photographer. Based in Vancouver, he has published several collections of his poems: Riding the Tide, Mirror of Dreams, A Kernel of Truth, Skipping Stones, Half Open Door and Lost in the Morning Calm. His poetry has been published in various literary magazines and anthologies.

Ashok is a Poet Laureate and poet ambassador to Japan, Korea and India. He is founder of WIN: Writers International Network Canada. Its main objective is to inspire, encourage, promote and recognize writers of diverse genres, artists and community leaders. He has received many accolades including Nehru Humanitarian Award for his leadership of Writers International Network Canada, Poets without Borders Peace Award for his journeys across the globe to celebrate peace and to create alliances with poets, and Kalidasa Award for creative writings.

Africa

Mother Africa
you are
birthplace of humanity.

Mediterranean and
Red Sea,
Atlantic and
Indian Ocean
wash your feet and body.

Mighty rivers
Nile, Congo, Niger, Zambezi and
many more
play in your lap.

Kilimanjaro stands
guard to you.
Lakes Victoria,
quenches
your thirst.

From your womb came
Europe, Americas,
Asia, Australia and
far flung islands.

The selfishness enslaved you,
chained your sons and daughters,
and traded them.

There you are flourishing
and blossoming again

after having
forgiven everyone.

After all you're
a kind mother
of humanity

Thank you,
Mother Africa.

Dolce Vita

Sometimes we just aren't
given a choice.

There is profound sadness
in full moon's blue cast.

It brings me joy
I never thought possible.

I seek from that joy
a direction to follow.

Unspoken

I wake up in my body and
it wasn't that body anymore.

There are days I give up on my body.
I think the life I want was the life
I have had.

I want to be the water clinging to your roots.

With both hands in the soil
I feel modesty of a new beginning
splendour of a tiny sprout
kneeling to the glory of God.

I hold it and wander
into the surge of forever
the unbroken time of infinity.

Ashok K. Bhargava

Caroline 'Ceri Naz' Nazareno

Carolin 'Ceri' Nazareno

Caroline Nazareno-Gabis a.k.a. Ceri Naz, born in Anda, Pangasinan known as a 'poet of peace and friendship', is a multi-awarded poet, journalist, editor, publicist, linguist, educator, and women's advocate.

Graduated cum laude with the degree of Bachelor of Elementary Education, specialized in General Science at Pangasinan State University. Ceri have been a voracious researcher in various arts, science and literature. She volunteered in Richmond Multicultural Concerns Society, TELUS World Science, Vancouver Art Gallery, and Vancouver Aquarium.

She was privileged to be chosen as one of the Directors of Writers Capital International Foundation (WCIF), Member of the Poetry Posse, one of the Board of Directors of Galaktika ATUNIS Magazine based in Albania; the World Poetry Canada and International Director to Philippines; Global Citizen's Initiatives Member, Association for Women's rights in Development (AWID) and Anacbanua. She has been a 4th Placer in World Union of Poets Poetry Prize 2016, Writers International Network-Canada ''Amazing Poet 2015'', The Frang Bardhi Literary Prize 2014 (Albania), the sair-gazeteci or Poet-Journalist Award 2014 (Tuzla, Istanbul, Turkey) and World Poetry Empowered Poet 2013 (Vancouver, Canada).

Dissent

I heard the languages of the poor,
The slaves and the black men
Tilling the soil,
Burnt lips, thick eyebrows and kinky hair,
Unfortunate hearts they seem.
It may take a hundred of face towels
To wipe their tears,
But not the injustice planted
Not the imprisoned fears
That left them hanging on their own
Grounds: hopeless, homeless moons.

Running The Race

the tiny lamp is the torch
when south meets north
with black and white horses
on the green mountains
running the race
of downfall
and heyday

the same hermano
from near and distant far
when left tells right
he was reborn
pleading on his bended knees
 founder of truth and
great poetry
he walks with barefoot—
vows nothing,
for he sees no one
but his true self.

yesterday

what's gone is not the ash of yesterday's impulses
call it once, twice or even thrice of repeated mysteries
the frequency of unexpected highs and lows
in the premises of unmistakable truths,
complete the existence in this four topsy turvy walls
wanting winner's wands to get inside fortune gates
there are prompt approvals, sometimes set to wait
listen to the sound of emptiness,
how it flows to the chants of tasteless chords,
how it burns the unwanted words,
how it goes to the channels of adversities
here now, spread the wings to the wind of strength.

Swapna Behera

Swapna Behera

Swapna Behera is a bilingual contemporary poet, author, translator and editor from Odisha, India .She was a teacher from 1984 to 2015 . Her stories, poems and articles are widely published in National and International journals, and ezines, and are translated into different national and International languages. She has penned four books. She was conferred upon the Prestigious International Poesis Award of Honor at the 2nd Bharat Award for Literature as Jury in 2015, The Enchanting Muse Award in India World Poetree Festival 2017, World Icon of Peace Award in 2017, and the Pentasi B World Fellow Poet in 2017.. She is the recipient of Gold Cross Of Wisdom Award ,the medal for The Best Teachers of the World from World Union of Poets in 2018, and The LIfe time Achievement Award ,The Best Planner Award, The Sahitya Shiromani Award, ATAL BiHARI BAJPAYEE AWARD 2018, Ambassador De Literature Award 2018 .She is the Ambassador of Humanity by Hafrikan Prince Art World Africa 2018 and an official member of World Nation's Writers Union ,Kazakhstan2018. At present she is the manager at Large, Planner and Columnist of The Literati, the administrator of several poetic groups ,the member of the Special Council of Five of World Union of Poets and the Cultural Ambassador of Inner Child Press U.S.

I Am Only Seven Mama ......!!!

These two months
Dear mama
You and me in the force -fed tent
You cooking couscous
Boiling camel's milk
And chicken soup
Adding calories to my body of seven
Thirty cheese purges
Those gargantuan calories
Your shouting to eat and drink continuously
Only at half an hour break !!
My belly swells   up like a balloon
To enhance my BMI; my curves
Or maybe you give some drugs which I don't know
Beaten by sticks
No play to grow my breasts
For man loves bumpy cheeks and fleshy body

Mama I feel sick
I vomit ,I cry
Am I a bulging puppet
I get diabetes ,heart disease
My kidney fails
Enough is enough mama
No more swallowing of food
Give them to my starving brothers
I want to live and play
I love life mama
My life is mine and not for the man
I kiss you to have pity on me

I am only seven mama ....
I love my life
Allow me to live my life ......

This poem is dedicated to the tiny girls those who suffer for Leblouh which is a practice of force feeding in Mauritania, Western Sahara and Southern Morocco. It is a taboo. Couscous is a staple pasta dish an important food of Africa

Swapna Behera

Dumb Sequences Of A Sunday

 sleepy morning ,cup of tea
a smile, a news paper
an amorous look
 hug in the kitchen
hot Paratha and tomato sauce
changing the calendar pages
incessant sizzling
of dimpled love
dumb sequences
marching forward on the ramp
blowing the trumpet
silently yet with glory
aha! dumb sequences
tickle, fickle, mingle, and zingle......
on a Sunday....

Paratha is a morning breakfast of India made up of wheat

The Zone Of My Sky

The zone of my feet
Is the melody
of the globe

The zone of my eyes
Is not the map
Or the shape
It is my dream

The zone of my hands
Is a[plate of rice
 to a refugee

The zone of my ears
Is the voice of tears
On the grin faces

The zone of my anthem
Is the heart beat of a butterfly
On the mast of a submarine

The zone of my sky
Is as luminous as
You and me .....

Swapna Behera

Albert 'Infinite' Carrasco

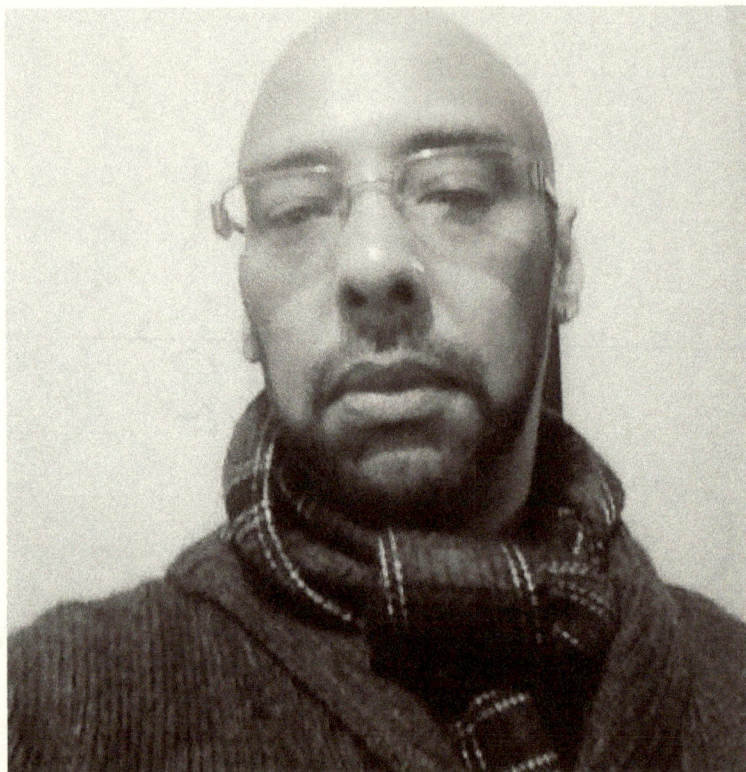

I'm a project life philanthropist, I speak about the non ethical treatment of poor ghetto people. Why? My family was their equal, my great grandmother and great grandfather was poor, my grandmother and grandfather, my mother and father, poverty to my family was a sequel, a traditional Inheritance of the subliminal. I paid attention to the decades of regression, i tried to make change, but when I came to the fork in the road and looked at the signs that read wrong < > right, I chose the left, the wrong direction, because of street life interactions a lot around me met death or incarceration. I failed myself and others. I regret my decisions, I can't reincarnate dead men, but I can give written visions in laymens. I'm back at that fork in the road, instead of it saying wrong or right, I changed it, now it says dead men < > life.

Infinite poetry @lulu.com

Alcarrasco2 on YouTube

Infinite the poet on reverbnation

Infinite Poetry

http://www.lulu.com/us/en/shop/al-infinite-carrasco/infinite-poetry/paperback/product-21040240.html

Central Africa

Bonjour
Como ce va
Nzoni gango
Bara mo Balaô
Greetings in French and Sango.
Hungry? You can enjoy rice,
Cassava,
Squash, pumpkin plantains,
Okra and Gombo
Melanin full skin glows with beauty,
Ears, necks noses and wrist accented with jewelry.
Traditional clothing include Pagne, agbada and Dashiki,
Tops and bottoms are cut from the same cloth to match
perfectly.
The Congo river,
Sahara,
Lake Chad and the Zambezi,
are a few of many places to go sightsee.

Don't go

Many men didn't want me to retire and raise my kids, that didn't suit em, that wasn't detrimental to their income, they wanted me to keep raising my children sauer along with smith and wesson for protection, it was beneficial to them if I stood in the hood buss'n mine and Chopin cookies to nickels and dimes. Ayo Inf I need about a six month run, I need you to hold me down in these trapped up slums, take a block by swingn that shit like a sword, let me and my team live and we'll pay you rent like a landlord, ayo inf can I get a shift, they needed money drip and godfather spliffs. I let em all eat, I wasn't turning my back on anyone, if I win we all won, plus I knew how hard it was to come up in these BX streets. I put that time in, put that work in, in the hood and the kitchen, I went through it all, got caked up, hit up, locked up, fell and came back up, plus, I buried most of the men with whom I came up. There was nothing left to witness but my own death, so I left before soul theft.

On point

If I didn't have gloves I used socks or rags to load my mags, had to make sure there was no prints on shells when protecting myself, kin, the trap and secured bags. Didn't wear fitted's, kept the darkies and my hoodie pulled tight, opp's couldn't give a descript they'll be like... all I saw was his nose and lips... I got to peek while he changed clips. It was ill times, had to live that way, you could thank god for waking you up then get blown away an hour later that day. As soon as you opened your eyes you had to live as if someone wanted you dead and any second they're going to try, I got hit, that shit hurts I can't lie, nikkas tried to leave me stiff as if I stared into Medusa's eyes, I was leaking watchn momma cry, told myself, inf you cant slip again, as soon as shit pops, let shit fly. Thru the years dudes sent in their hit men, I sent back aviation, they never came back, that's message confirmation. The streets made me a beast, skills got better but my anger got worse, couldn't be everywhere at the same time, I could've prevented flatlines instead of following hearse after hearse.

Eliza Segiet

Eliza Segioet

After earning a Master's Degree in Philosophy at the Jagiellonian University in Krakaw, Poland, Eliza Segiet proceeded with her post-graduate studies in the fields of Cultural Knowledge, Penal Revenue and Economic Criminal Law, Arts and Literature and Film and Television Production in the Polish city, Lodz.

With specific regard to her creative writings, the author describes herself as being torn in her passion for engaging in two literary genres: Poetry and Drama. A similar dichotomy from within is reflected on Segiet's own words about her true nature: She likes to look at the clouds, but she keeps both of her feet set firmly on the ground.

The author describes her worldview as being in harmony with that of Arthur Schopenhauer: "Ordinary people merely think how they shall 'spend' their time; a man of talent tries to 'use' it".

To Have Less

In the evening
through the alleys
seeps the music,
Cesária Évora's voice

delights and calms.

Joy is painted
on the faces.

Here everything is:
- *no problem,*
- *no stress.*

Sunk in delight,
nowhere do they see evil,
they do not share time

– it is theirs.

Tangled problems
become nothing.

Here they understood
that to have less
means
to be more.

Locals

In the sun,
flicker the golden sands of the beaches.
Around the earth scorched from the heat
– patches of color,
evoking the name of the islands.

Fields and hotel plazas
turning green,
bodies of the newcomers
turning brown.

Smiling locals
point out
how little you need
to enjoy the moment.

How little,
– to discover
joy in yourself.

Totem

The builder and the destroyer,
the thinking and the thoughtless
leaves behind a trace of
plastic
a totem of the present.

William S.
Peters Sr.

Bill's writing career spans a period of over 50 years. Being first Published in 1972, Bill has since went on to Author in excess of 40 additional Volumes of Poetry, Short Stories, etc., expressing his thoughts on matters of the Heart, Spirit, Consciousness and Humanity. His primary focus is that of Love, Peace and Understanding!

Bill says . . .

I have always likened Life to that of a Garden. So, for me, Life is simply about the Seeds we Sow and Nourish. All things we "Think and Do", will "Be" Cause and eventually manifest itself to being an "Effect" within our own personal "Existences" and "Experiences" . . . whether it be Fruit, Flowers, Weeds or Barren Landscapes! Bill highly regards the Fruits of his Labor and wishes that everyone would thus go on to plant "Lovely" Seeds on "Good Ground" in their own Gardens of Life!

to connect with Bill, he is all things Inner Child

www.iaminnerchild.com

Personal Web Site

www.iamjustbill.com

Africa

I have walked the sand of my ancestors
That were once flooded
With the blood and tears
Of conquest

The foreigner came upon us
With bibles
And strange tongue
And ideas
That we had no use of

They vied,
Coveted
That which our Creator
Provided,
And we had no concerns,
For greed was not
Of our way,
So we gave,
And we gave
And we became the slave
To their avarice

From North to South,
East to West
Our souls were tested
And to this day
The way of these men
Has not changed

For why did our Creator

Make us so trusting,
Unsuspecting
And forgiving . . .

Is there not enough
For every one
In . . . Africa ?

How Long?

How long is 1/2 of forever?

My people have suffered,
Endured and tolerated
Via fronts of slavery and racism
Far too long.
Though we are not the only ones
Throughout humanity's history,
I must admit my conscious diaspora
Is cuttinlgy acute,
To the white meat of my soul . . .
And it ain't cute!

How long is 1/2 of forever?

We have been praying
To this God you gave us
That you stole from the Jews
To manipulate, mold and shape,
To implement and use as you choose
Which includes the White Jesus from Africa
But he ain't hearing this Black Slave's pleas
Even though I reverently fold my hands
And fall to my knees,
Begging "please, help me"
As I make my decrees
For myself,
My children,
My family,
My people,
Humanity.

I wonder . . .

Have you made God
In your own image? . . .
Has God, too, now become
A misogynist,
Homo-phobic,
Secular,
Exclusionary,
Racist?

How long is 1/2 of forever?

I/we
Have been holding on
For how long now?
When will I/we get served?
Please call my number
Let me/we walk through the front doors
Of equality,
Justice,
Opportunity,
Humanity.

How long is 1/2 of forever?

I/we
Are tired of sneaking in the back door
To receive what little crumbs
You choose to afford us.

How long is 1/2 of forever?

We will no longer apply for the ration
Of the fruit
From the Garden of Creation
That we deserve.

William S. Peters, Sr.

Are we not all Children of
The same Creator?

How long is 1/2 of forever?

Lord, Lord, Lord Jesus,
I'm holding on,
Still singing that same old
Soul-worn song,
"We Shall Overcome".

How long?

How long is 1/2 of forever?
'Cause I'm tired of this shit!

Critique

The pool where tears were spawned from
Was beginning to empty
And the eyes which shed them
Was beginning to grow weary
Of all that they have witnessed
In this life-time

It seemed as if
There was a virus abound
Infecting the reason of men
And women too

Children no longer had a dependable path
Available to them
That led to a balanced adulthood
For the ones who were responsible
For their charge
Were maligned by
The discordantly skewed ways
Of the world

Oh Lorde, what are we to do?

People of color
Being attacked
For being colorful,
For standing out
Because of their melanin
Which is proudly on display

Yes, Black is beautiful,
But many see it as a threat,
A blight on humanity

A nuisance
That disturbs their
False solace

BTW, you are beautiful too
Regardless of your hued-ness
Or lack thereof

Some would rather embrace
And project their ugliness
On our world
That could be so much more
Than what it is we see,
Or tend to focus on

When will reason assail
Where reason fails ?

I have hopes,
As do my children,
My people
And my ancestors

Can we not some day express
Our divinity
Beyond the errant trinity
You have indoctrinated us with . . .
Superiority, Privilege & Prejudice

I have looked to your God,
Prayed to your God,
Cried to your God,
And there is no intervention
That brings a cease
To the demise

Or brings rise
To the deceased
Who have died needlessly
By your hand . . .
And continue to do so

And I must say . . .
It is not only I and we
But many across the globe
Who suffer your indulgence
Of GREED

There is of course . . .
Palestine,
Afghanistan,
Syria,
Iraq,
Libya,
Darfur,
Yemen,
Sudan,
And all of Africa
And soon to be Iran
And all of man
And those who have yet to stand
And rebuke your avarice

This is not much of a movement in verse
But a terse critique . . .

I hope you read this
And reason
Like a phoenix

Is resurrected
From its grave

Not every poem needs to be about Flowers and Butterflies .
. .
This poem was written about Love and the lack thereof.

April

2019

Features

~ * ~

D L Davis

Michelle Joan Barulich

Lulëzim Haziri

Fakleeha Hassan

i Fly

because

I Can

... said the Dreamer to the world.

www.iamjustbill.com

116

D L
Davis

D.L. began his poetic journey in 1987. D.L. ranked 3rd Place in the 2010 San Diego Poetry Slam competition & co-hosted the internet poetry radio show, Xpressions Radio - Bad Boys Kitchen (2010 National Poetry Award Winner).

D.L.'s favorite artist is Prince and he enjoys listening to smooth jazz music.

D.L.'s first book release, "My Soul Told Me To" is available @ www.amazon.com/author/dldavisthepoet

D.L. believes, "life itself is an immeasurable source of inspiration, just KEEP AN OPEN MIND AND INSPIRATION WILL COME TO YOU"

In The Name Of Poetry, Amen

Connect with D.L. - dldavisthepoet on FB, IG & Twitter

BLACK TAX

When I was young, my life was worth $5
I raised my hand when I needed to be excused Due to
inflation, my life is worth $10
I raise both hands falsely accused Kill that nigger! No
excuses!
Somehow my surrender stand resembles a b-boy battle
stance Will the war on black boys ever end?

Freeze! Don't move!
I was standing still, hands up On the ground!
I was kneeling, fingers laced behind my head I was spread
eagle and face down
No matter what position I assumed,
I was presumed guilty and my innocence, never had chance

Why? Is the battle cry that echoes across cold toes in the
middle of hot streets; just another tar baby from the cradle
to the grave

We catch bullets in the streets and our backyards like,
we catch footballs and baseballs in the streets and our
backyards Brown bodies found on street corners are
common like,
brown paper bags found on street corners;
just trash waiting for a cool breeze to blow them into
hashtags

There's a name that goes with this face I'm a book whose
story has yet been told I'm God's grace, under your fire
I've seen this move. I know how it unfolds. This does not
end well for me

Let's change the narrative. That's what we can do I won't
move. You don't shoot
I just want to get home, alive and in one piece just like you

GOOD LOVE

To me, GOOD LOVE is honesty
Saying "J'adore Toi" with conviction Being looked at with
the sincerest eyes Being doc or nurse when your partner is
ill
Being held in the warmest and most caring arms Being
spoken to in the softest voice
Buying flowers or cards just because
Writing sweet messages on a post-it then put it in a place
you know your partner will find it

To me, GOOD LOVE is holding hands ever so gently
and yet nothing can break that bind because the love that
holds it together is 100x stronger than super-duper glue
The soft, full-contact kisses that leave you breathless, weak
in the knees and still yearning for more
Laughing and crying together
Bringing out the best in each other; a partnership

GOOD LOVE is more than using certain body parts to give
and receive sexual pleasure GOOD LOVE is loving from
your heart and loving your partner for what is in his or hers

HAVE YOU HAD YOUR GOOD LOVE TODAY?

TIME

If I had one wish
I'd wish to go back in TIME, and this TIME I would not
rush into a relationship
I would use that TIME to become all that I can be And love
me for me

I would not take TIME for granted
I would take advantage of TIME and spend more
TIME with the seeds I planted so they would grow strong
roots and exude an undeniable sense of self and prosper

TIME, oh TIME, where
Where art thou precious, TIME?
You said you were on my side, but I look around and
you're nowhere to be found Where have you gone, oh
unforgiving, TIME?

In my dreams I hear you ticking away
I run towards your call but I can't seem to catch up to you
With bated breath and all my might, I run
I run and run and run and…I'm running

…out of TIME

Michelle Joan Barulich

Michelle Joan Barulich

Hi My name is Michelle Joan Barulich and I have enjoyed writing poetry and songs for many years. I am published in several poetry books by Watermark Press. I am currently studying the Alternative Medicine. I have 3 rescued pet pigeons that have brought me a lot of joy. Thank you Inner Child Press you have made a lot of people happy by letting people write and enjoy other
people's poetry.

My Web link:
www.facebook.com/michelle.barulich

Whispers of Eternity

…And you say were the radicals
This world is filled with answers
Open up your eyes
Throw all your manmade lies
I need no man to bring out the best in me
My life is on the run
Like a whisper from eternity
I don't live by your rules
Of the hand and mind
And I see the tide of the change
You made us to believe
That their is no hope
I'm not another victim to believe
Their is still time to heed
Your so damn predictable
In everything that you do
..And I see the tide of the change
I'm still here waiting for you
For you, and I wait so long for you, for you....

12:12

Twelve-twelve is a number
That I'm always seeing all around
Help me so I can understand
Sociology, Biology
We're all complicated
By the words we hear
But in the truth its what lyes in the soul
Physiology, Psychology
If you love me, you will be here
And if you don't, then you won't show
Philosophy, Cryptography
Lessons to be learned in this world
Takes a lot of patience
Caring for the solution, may sometime make it worse
Mythology, Geology
Does this strange Phantom exist?
Light your cigarette and show me where the smoke rings go
Stimulation, Revelation
Prophet telling, go ahead I'm listening
Books will make you wise
Michelle dreamed that she was in a play
I awoke suddenly, to see 12:12 staring at me
Does the thinker always know
And does question mark
Understand why its asking?
12:12 help me so I can understand.....

Bittersweet

And now you're tellin' me
That my love runs too deep
And then you're tellin' me
I'm coming on too strong
Isn't life funny?
And you spend all of my money
And call it bittersweet
..And then your tellin' me
I'm not paying enough attention to your needs
And then you're tellin' me
I can't be reached
What do you want me to do?
What are you looking for in me?
I have a heart that needs to be filled
With your kindness and love
But you turn it all around on me
..And now you're tellin' me
That I'm asking for too much
And then you're tellin' me
That you can't live without my touch
Isn't life funny?
How he calls it, so bittersweet....

Lulëzim Haziri

Lulëzim Haziri is a poet that lives in a city in the Republic of North Macedonia

He is also a Korespodent · 1992 to present · Gostivar

No further information submitted.

Please visit his FaceBook Page for more information
www.facebook.com/lulzim.haziri

The one fish in the aquarium
prologue

the flora from this side of the window makes you see
long faces with bulging eyes
staring ironically
you ask yourself
who brought it into this aquarium
or did it enter by itself
running away from the golden hook
so much time has passed
that it does not remember any longer

(this is called solitude)
you wander in the streets to meet somebody
suddenly you catch your self talking to the windows
with the leaves and the sun
head down (love sinner) you find that you are
running to the well known path
with trousers wet from the morning dew
while the blissful world is sipping coffee indolently
you clutch onto your key in your pocket
all rusty from perspiration
that could not possibly open a single door
or key holes or ears or lips all grown with moss
times when doors are opened with bells

(and this is called solitude)
standing behind the bar he orders two glasses
the barman finds it difficult to talk and drink at the
same time
having counted all drinks in the glass buffet
while his paths intertwine beneath his feet
he fixes his eyes at the door with a lost glance
awaiting vigorous words
to cure his head like an aspirin

(this is nothing else but solitude)
he leaves the entrance door wide open
lingering hanging and counting gates
like a jacket on a hanger
waiting for a notice or inditement
he has so much to say but to whom
his tongue is numb from the juice of the words
spiders have raptured his fingers on the keyboard
windows are sealed

(this is solitude not creativity)
at the working table eaten up by worms
he sits down to write about pain about evidence
letters march like black ants
eating up his paper like a cookie
he throws paper at them over and over again
treating them like late guests

Translated by Robert Alagjozoski

Hamburg 92
St. Pauli

can the impotence of moral be cured
in flats full of chandeliers
incest stinking girls
exposing their young breasts to their fathers
voyeur mothers peeping at their masturbating sons
spreading adour St. Pauli all over the world
this pornographic Mecca of frustrations
sewages clogged with menstruation
whores standing in the rain
master performance under
complex conditions of
-10 degrees Celsius hanging about in knickers
diligent workers imaging
the all the flowers of Hamburg picked
for their processions
they earn with disgust and spend with hope
prices are not high in St. Pauli
you can haggle with only a smile
and get it cheaper than in Amsterdam
they pay confused
fake sighs cannot stop them
surface that the hens of St. Pauli do not lay eggs
they enter with closed eyes through the same gates
not to be seen by Hades pimps
only when they come out they are dressed as turks
hindus Albanians Vietnamese ermanians zanzibari
Japanese with cameras around their necks…

subway
how much money do you have in pocket
will you steal our mother's wallet

how much money do you have in pocket
on a trip to India can you set off
how much money do you have in pocket
soft joint or cocaine
how much money do you have in pocket
blood transfusion has become so expensive
how much money do you have in pocket
to a Turk would you sell your young body
how much money do you have in pocket
… thousaaands staresssss…
….thousaaaands mirrooooors….
…thousaaaands waaaaves I seeee….
how much money do you have in pocket
red lipstick for astrological signs
on the subway walls you waste for nothing
how much money do you have in pocket
the daylight dreams has become so expensive
how much money do you have in pocket…

kings of lager
with darkness under the old jacket
he clings on like a somnambulist
following sleepless taxi lights
trying to dissipate the night into dawn
slumberous post lamps
throw stones at him from above
nothing makes him return to his bed
with extinguished passion underneath
like dirty laundry all forgotten
streets seem endless without pavements
while rolling down the steps of the underground
his jacket protects him from harm
where he falls he surrenders a bit to his sleep
with one eye closed he thinks about his wife

Lulëzim Haziri

watching over their children
counting dream pearls with a faint voice
and a pencil that does nor remember the numbers
calculating the drinks for tomorrow
darkness has conquered his eyes
and covered the inside of all bars
thus he talks to the sky

Translated by Robert Alagjozosk

Winter and Other Seasons

I. When I start on a long journey in spring
I forget you oh my quiet home
I travel from one foreign land to another
Like from one woman to another
I travel through lands that take me in from the front door
The way young brides take in their sweet-talking lovers
But you remain in the silence of a woman waiting for her
husband
Faithful and broken by his harshness
You are a wife who looks after her unborn children
A woman who takes love but gives nothing in return
I ask for one brittle kiss
One gentle look
Or one touch

II.
When I start on a long journey in summer
I remember you first oh my sweating home
You are slower than the turtle and the snail
I know you meditate with your legs crossed
I know your silence like a hermit
Who's given up love's delight
Nothing changes in you
The same sky is above you, the same season
Your walls are indifferent as usual
Change for you is an trala-la-laaa

III.
When I depart from you in autumn
You disappear from my sight, my colourful home
You don't have the grey face of the European homes
The ashen shade I see in the small cloud above the coffee
cups

Lulëzim Haziri

Wherever I drink one
No one knows to buy you clothes
They take wrong measures
They don't care about your taste
The fashion designers dress you in childish colours
Your character differs from the clothes you wear
Your stubbornness turns into a rebellious silence
As never before you now need a new architect like Sinan
Who'd make me return to your embrace

IV.
And in winter, in winter I can't escape from you
You stick like slush on my trouser-legs
Your whiteness is blinding but I don't wear sun glasses
I am happy when you light up my body
when your clarity blinds my eyes
When I return to the room to warm my feet
When the kettle steam excites my nostrils
When I close the cracks of the windows and the feelings
To prevent the entry of the cold
When I tie my head to the body with a woollen scarf
When I put my frozen hands into your warm pockets
When I seek and find a planetary harmony in every detail
When I throw away the cares like an empty cigarette box
Winter is a heavenly season
A season of the gods
My season
So please don't cast me out of your warm womb

Translated by Zoran Anceski

Faleeha Hassan

She is a widely celebrated poet, teacher, editor, writer, playwriter born in Najaf, Iraq, in 1967, who now lives in the United States.

Faleeha is the first woman to wrote poetry for children in Iraq. She received her master's degree in Arabic literature, and has now published 20 books. Her poems have been translated into English, Turkmen, Bosevih, Indian, French, Italian, German, Kurdish, Spain, Korean, Greek and Albanian. Ms. Hassan has received many awards in Iraq and throughout the Middle East for her poetry and short stories.

Faleeha Hassan has also had her poems and short stories published in a variety of American magazines such as: Philadelphia poets 22, Harbinger Asylum, Brooklyn Rail April2016, Screaming mamas, The Galway Review, Words Without Borders, TXTOBJX, Intranslation, SJ Magazine, Nondoc, Wordgathering , SCARLET LEAF REVIEW, Courier-Post, I am not a Silent Poet, Taos Journal, Inner Child Press, Atlantic City Press, SJ Magazine, Intranslation Magazine, The Guardian, Words Without Borders, Courier-Post, Life and Legends, Wordgathering, SCARLET LEAF REVIEW, Indiana Voice Journal, The Bees Are Dead, IWA, Poetry Soup, Poetry Adelaide Literary Magazine, Philly, The Fountain Magazine, DRYLAND, The Blue Mountain Review, Otoliths, Taos Journal of Poetry and Art, TXTOBJX, DODGING THE RAIN, Poetry Adelaide Literary Magazine, NonDoc Philly, DRYLAND, American Poetry Review, The Fountain Magazine, Uljana Wolf, Arcs, Tiferet and Ice Cream Poetry Anthology , Dryland Los Angeles underground art &writing Magazine , Opa Anthology of contemporary , BACOPA Literary Review , Better than Starbucks Magazine , Tweymatikh ZQH Magazine ,TUCK Magazine and Street Light Press

Email : d.fh88@yahoo.com

My Guest

There is nothing more important than you, my guest
I will delay my sickness until you leave
And I will cover my sadness with a big smile
I will give my last bread to you and my hungry kids
Don't worry--
I will fill my stomach with water
Come on in...
My house is full of the incense of hospitality
Its walls are made of peace
I know one thing--
You are not my guest
You are my blessing from my God
Don't tell me your name
or
Where you come from
or
Why you are here
After three days
When you leave my house
We will shake hands with hope for the next visit.

After forty years of snow

Do you remember the watch you gave to me wrapped in a
poem?
It is still bound to my soul's meaning
The more time passes
The more the letters jump into my heart artery
My heart is now pumping flirtation
How many times I have wished
That if my city were not surrounded by graves
Then like a little girl
I would wait for you in a secret garden
Come on!
Take off this thick absence
As thick as a New Jersey coat in the winter time
Melt off the snow that has stacked on the lines of your
messages
Mow the grass that has grown on your tongue
Don't save a sea of tears for me
I am not a mermaid
Make yourself present with words
Woo me
Let me stop demanding my rights
And thrive by the touch of your fingers as they play with
my hair
Let me fool myself again
And see you as center of my universe

Faleeha Hassan

When I drink tea in New Jersey

Like a girl who writes poetry about a boy she has never
seen
My day sits with all this disappointment
Counting her fleeting moments
 I remember my mother using the smell of onions
 To shed her tears in the kitchen
For the absence of my father
 Who climbed his life war by war
Whenever he wore his military belt
 He wished that war was just an old shoe
He could take it off whenever he liked
And he didn't need to think of fixing it at the cobbler's shop
I remember my brother
Who asked in his letters--
When will the war understand that we are not good at
dealing with death?
I remember us forty years ago
We were kids, very much kids
With colorful clothes and hearts
It was enough for us to see a balloon
To drown in big laughter
I remember all this now
When I drink my tea
And
I practice my loneliness.

Remembering

our fallen soldiers of verse

Janet Perkins Caldwell
February 14, 1959 ~ September 20, 2016

Alan W. Jankowski
16 March 1961 ~ 10 March 2017

Inner Child Press

News

We are so excited to share and announce a few of the current books, as well as the new and upcoming books of some of our Poetry Posse authors.

On the following pages we present to you ...

Jackie Davis Allen

Gail Weston Shazor

hülya n. yılmaz

Nizar Sartawi

Faleeha Hassan

Fahredin Shehu

Caroline 'Ceri' Nazareno

Eliza Segiet

William S. Peters, Sr.

Now Available at
www.innerchildpress.com

Now Available at
www.innerchildpress.com

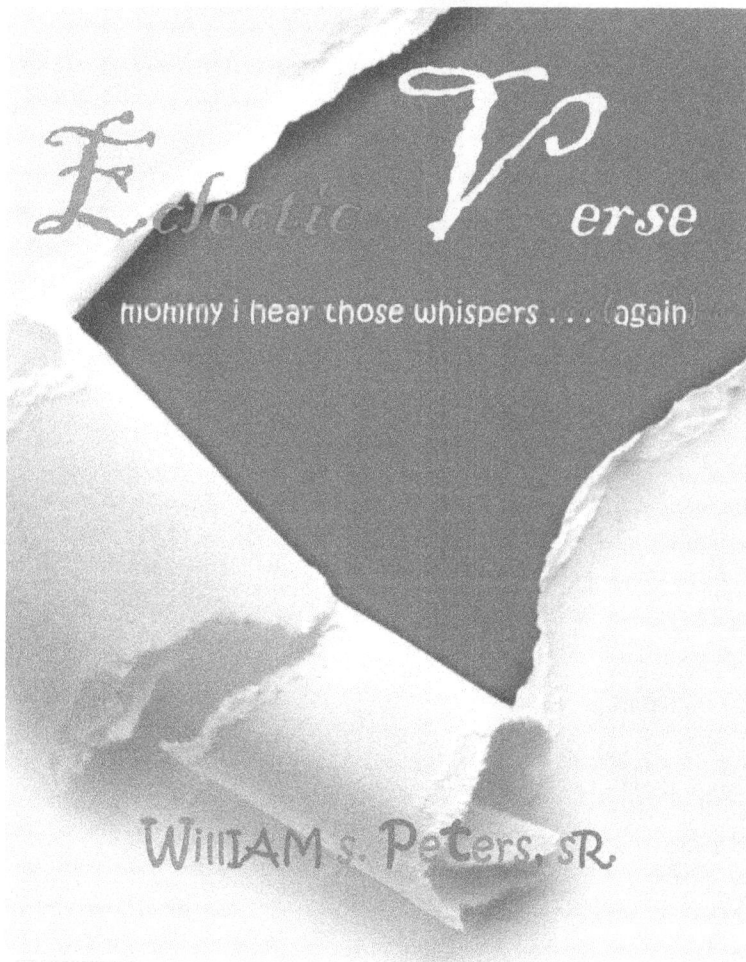

Inner Child Press News

Now Available at
www.innerchildpress.com

HERENOW

FAHREDIN SHEHU

Now Available at
www.innerchildpress.com

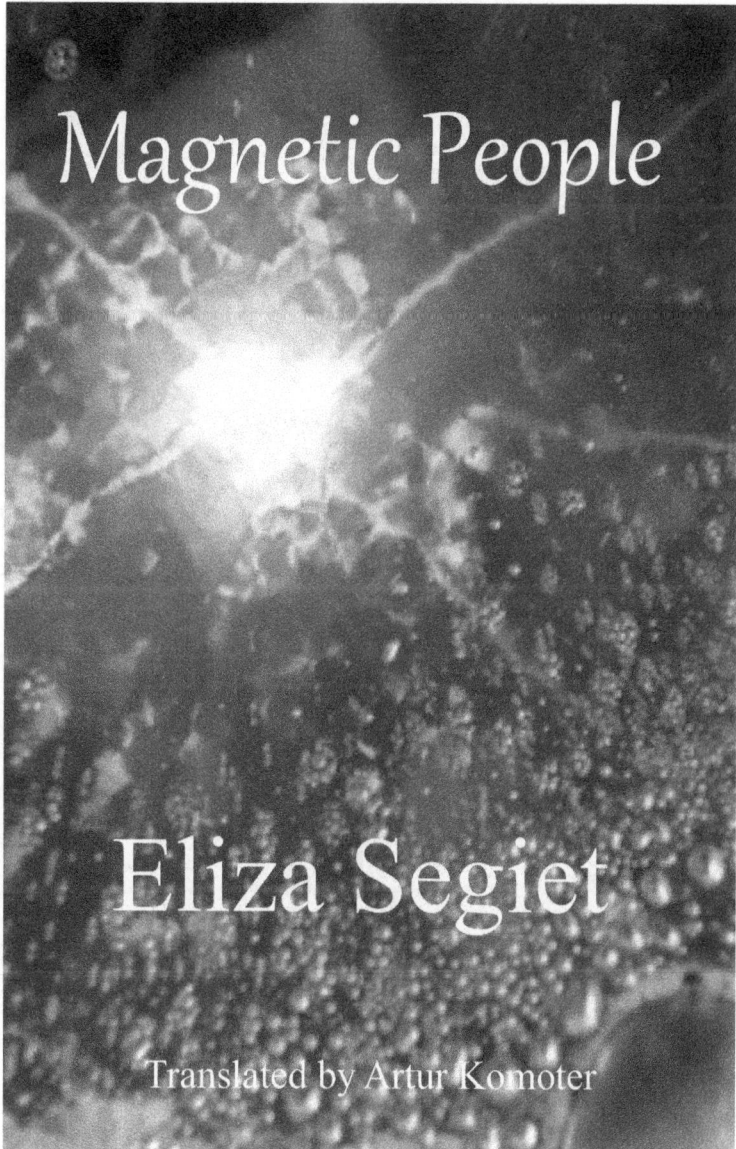

Magnetic People

Eliza Segiet

Translated by Artur Komoter

Now Available at
www.innerchildpress.com

Now Available at
www.innerchildpress.com

Lies
My
Grandfathers
Told
Me

Gail Weston Shazor

Now Available at
www.innerchildpress.com

Aflame

Memoirs in Verse

hülya n. yılmaz

Now Available at
www.innerchildpress.com

My Shadow

Nizar Sartawi

Inner Child Press News

Now Available at
www.innerchildpress.com

Mass Graves

Faleeha Hassan

The Year of the Poet VI ~ April 2019

Now Available at
www.innerchildpress.com

Breakfast

for

Butterflies

Faleeha Hassan

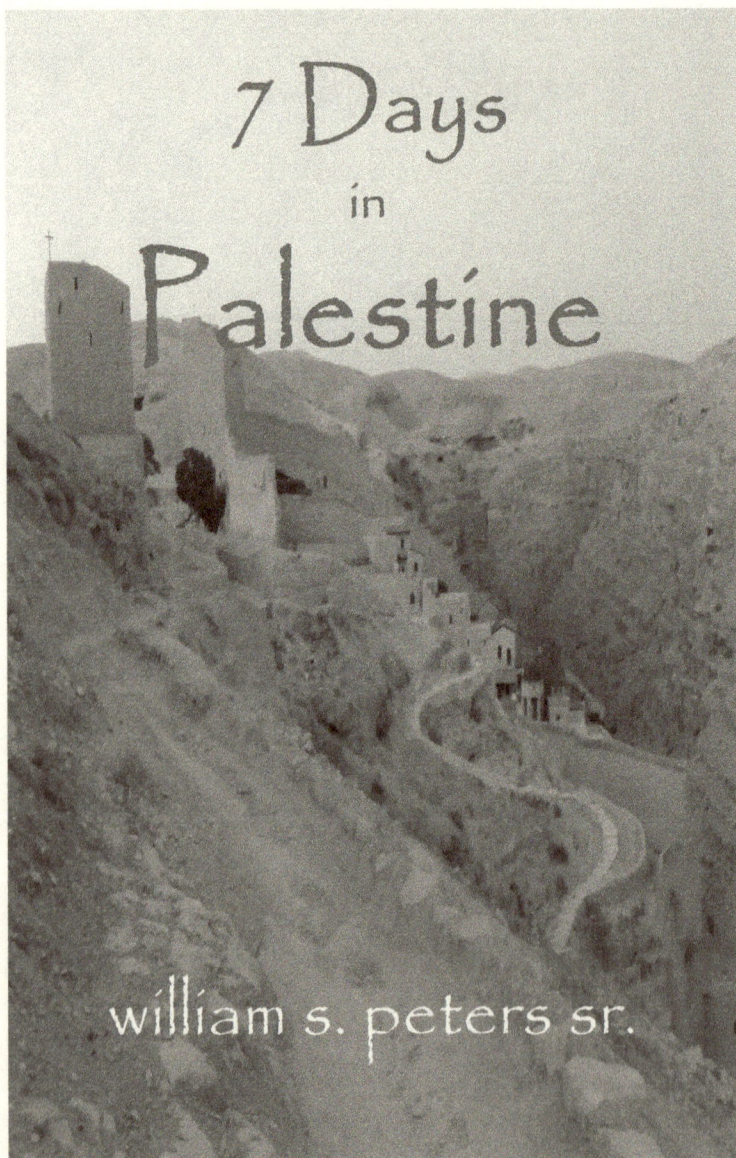

7 Days in Palestine
william s. peters sr.

Now Available at
www.innerchildpress.com

inner child press
presents

Tunisia My Love

william s. peters, sr.

Coming in the Summer of 2019

The Journey

Footprints and Shadows

Kosovo
Tunisia
Macedonia
Morocco
Jordan
Palestine
Israel
Italy
Turkey

a collection of poetry inspired during my travels

william s. peters, sr.

Now Available at
www.innerchildpress.com

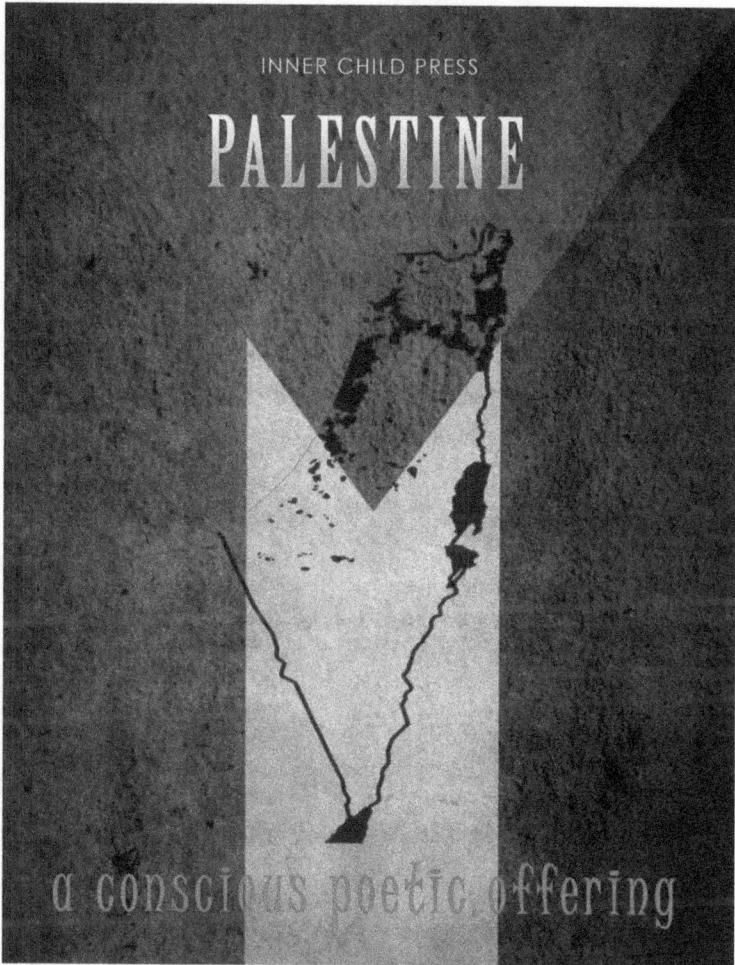

Now Available at

www.innerchildpress.com

Think on These Things
Book II

william s. peters, sr.

Now Available at
www.innerchildpress.com

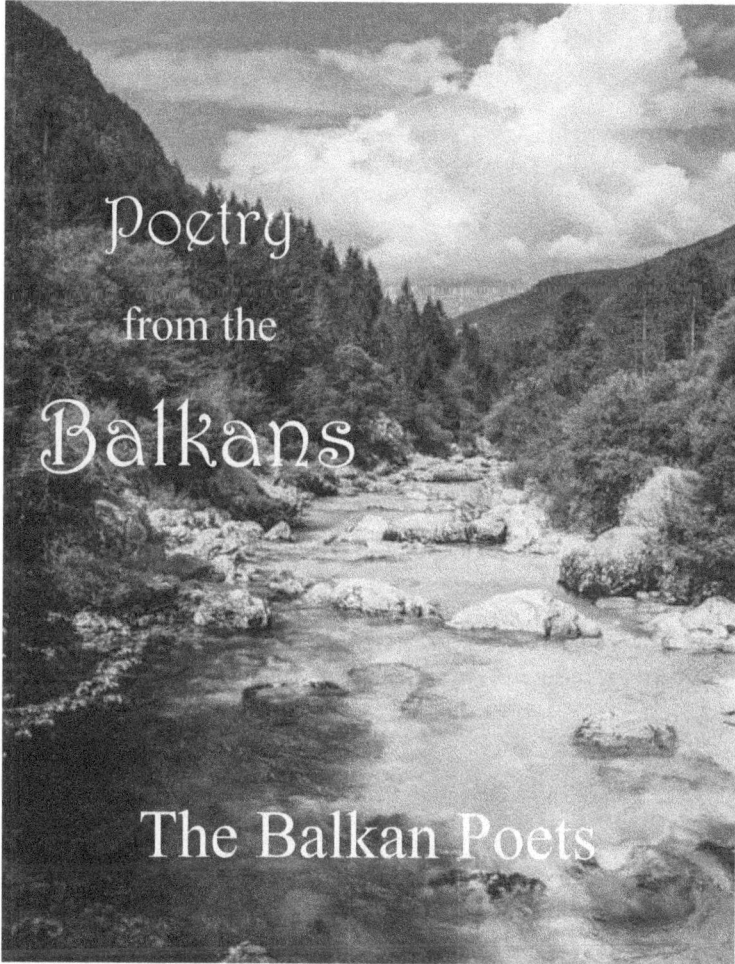

Poetry
from the
Balkans

The Balkan Poets

Other

Anthological

works from

Inner Child Press International

www.innerchildpress.com

Inner Child Press International
presents

A Love Anthology

2019

The Love Poets

Now Available

www.worldhealingworldpeacepoetry.com

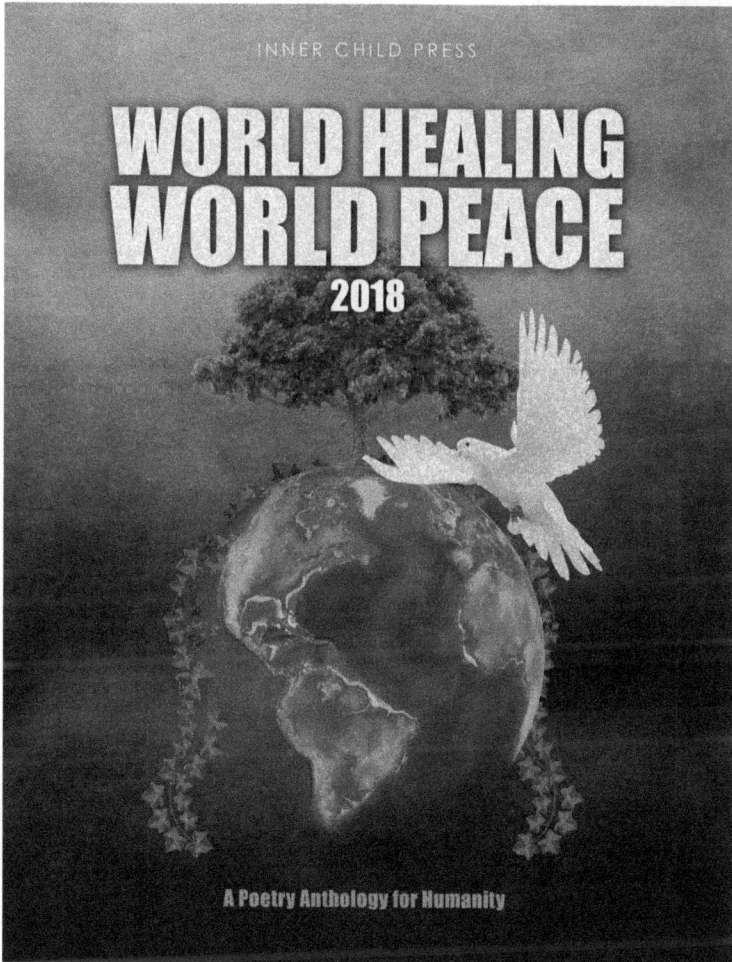

INNER CHILD PRESS

WORLD HEALING
WORLD PEACE
2018

A Poetry Anthology for Humanity

Now Available

www.worldhealingworldpeacepoetry.com

172

Now Available

www.innerchildpress.com/anthologies

Now Available

healing through words

Poetry ... Prose ... Prayer ... Stories

Janet

gone too soon . . .

a
Poetically
Spoken
Anthology
volume I
Collector's Edition

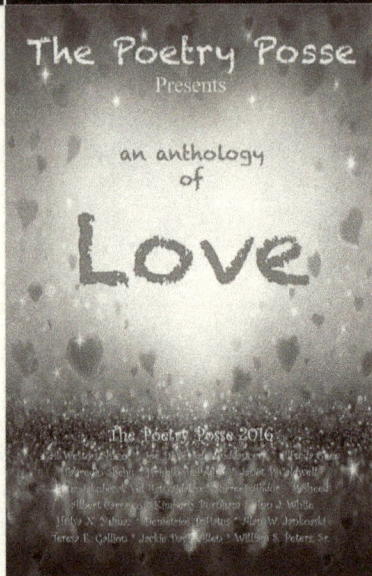

The Poetry Posse
Presents

an anthology
of

Love

The Poetry Posse 2016

Now Available

www.innerchildpress.com/anthologies

176

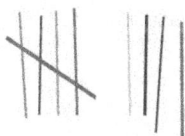

Now Available

www.innerchildpress.com/anthologies

The Year of the Poet
January 2014

The Poetry Posse

Jamie Bond
Gail Weston Shazor
Albert 'Infinite' Carrasco
Siddartha Beth Pierce
Janet P. Caldwell
June 'Bugg' Barefield
Debbie M. Allen
Tony Henninger
Joe DaVerbal Minddancer
Robert Gibbons
Neetu Wali
Shareef Abdur-Rasheed
William S. Peters, Sr.

Carnation

Our January Feature
Terri L. Johnson

the Year of the Poet
February 2014

violets

The Poetry Posse

Jamie Bond
Gail Weston Shazor
Albert 'Infinite' Carrasco
Siddartha Beth Pierce
Janet P. Caldwell
June 'Bugg' Barefield
Debbie M. Allen
Tony Henninger
Joe DaVerbal Minddancer
Robert Gibbons
Neetu Wali
Shareef Abdur-Rasheed
William S. Peters, Sr.

Our February Features
Teresa E. Gallion & Robert Gibson

the Year of the Poet
March 2014

The Poetry Posse

Jamie Bond
Gail Weston Shazor
Albert 'Infinite' Carrasco
Siddartha Beth Pierce
Janet P. Caldwell
June 'Bugg' Barefield
Debbie M. Allen
Tony Henninger
Joe DaVerbal Minddancer
Robert Gibbons
Neetu Wali
Shareef Abdur-Rasheed
Kimberly Burnham
William S. Peters, Sr.

daffodil

Our March Featured Poets
AliciaC. Cooper & hülya yılmaz

the Year of the Poet
April 2014

The Poetry Posse

Jamie Bond
Gail Weston Shazor
Albert 'Infinite' Carrasco
Siddartha Beth Pierce
Janet P. Caldwell
June 'Bugg' Barefield
Debbie M. Allen
Tony Henninger
Joe DaVerbal Minddancer
Robert Gibbons
Neetu Wali
Shareef Abdur-Rasheed
Kimberly Burnham
William S. Peters, Sr.

Our April Featured Poets
Fahredin Shehu
Martina Reisz Newberry
Justin Blackburn
Monte Smith

Sweet Pea

celebrating international poetry month

Now Available

www.innerchildpress.com/the-year-of-the-poet

the year of the poet
May 2014

May's Featured Poets
ReeCee
Joski the Poet
Shannon Stanton

Dedicated To our Children

The Poetry Posse
Jamie Bond
Gail Weston Shazor
Albert Infinite' Carrasco
Siddartha Beth Pierce
Janet P. Caldwell
June 'Bugg' Barefield
Debbie M. Allen
Tony Henninger
Joe DaVerbal Straddlancer
Robert Gibbons
Neetu Wali
Shareef Abdur Rasheed
Kimberly Burnham
William S. Peters, Jr.

Lily of the Valley

the Year of the Poet
June 2014

Love & Relationship

Rose

June's Featured Poets
Shantelle McLin
Jacqueline D. E. Kennedy
Abraham N. Benjamin

The Poetry Posse
Jamie Bond
Gail Weston Shazor
Albert 'Infinite' Carrasco
Siddartha Beth Pierce
Janet P. Caldwell
June 'Bugg' Barefield
Debbie M. Allen
Tony Henninger
Joe DaVerbal Minddance
Robert Gibbons
Neetu Wali
Shareef Abdur-Rasheed
Kimberly Burnham
William S. Peters, Sr.

The Year of the Poet
July 2014

July Feature Poets
Christena A. V. Williams
Dr. John R. Strum
Kolade Olanrewaju Freedom

The Poetry Posse
Jamie Bond
Gail Weston Shazor
Albert 'Infinite' Carrasco
Siddartha Beth Pierce
Janet P. Caldwell
June 'Bugg' Barefield
Debbie M. Allen
Tony Henninger
Joe DaVerbal Minddance
Robert Gibbons
Neetu Wali
Shareef Abdur-Rasheed
Kimberly Burnham
William S. Peters, Sr.

Lotus
Asian Flower of the Month

The Year of the Poet
August 2014

Gladiolus

The Poetry Posse
Jamie Bond
Gail Weston Shazor
Albert 'Infinite' Carrasco
Siddartha Beth Pierce
Janet P. Caldwell
June 'Bugg' Barefield
Debbie M. Allen
Tony Henninger
Joe DaVerbal Minddance
Robert Gibbons
Neetu Wali
Shareef Abdur-Rasheed
Kimberly Burnham
William S. Peters, Sr.

August Feature Poets
Ann White * Rosalind Cherry * Sheila Jenkins

Now Available

www.innerchildpress.com/the-year-of-the-poet

The Year of the Poet
September 2014

Aster   Morning-Glory

Wild Child of September Birthday Flower

September Feature Poets
Florence Malone * Keith Alan Hamilton

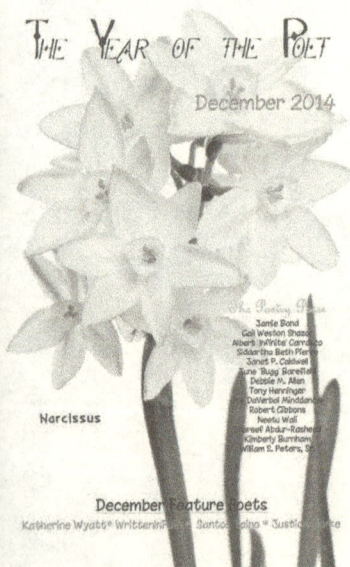

The Poetry Posse
Jamie Bond * Gail Weston Shazor * Albert 'Infinite' Carrasco * Siddartha Beth Pierce
Janet P. Caldwell * June 'Bugg' Barefield * Debbie M. Allen * Tony Henninger
Joe DaVerbal Minddancer * Robert Gibbons * Neetu Wali * Shareef Abdur-Rasheed
Kimberly Burnham * William S. Peters, Sr.

THE YEAR OF THE POET
October 2014

Red Poppy

The Poetry Posse
Jamie Bond * Gail Weston Shazor * Albert 'Infinite' Carrasco * Siddartha Beth Pierce
Janet P. Caldwell * June 'Bugg' Barefield * Debbie M. Allen * Tony Henninger
Joe DaVerbal Minddancer * Robert Gibbons * Neetu Wali * Shareef Abdur-Rasheed
Kimberly Burnham * William S. Peters, Sr.

October Feature Poets
Ceri Naz * RaJendra Padini * Elizabeth Castillo

THE YEAR OF THE POET
November 2014

Chrysanthemum

The Poetry Posse
Jamie Bond * Gail Weston Shazor * Albert 'Infinite' Carrasco * Siddartha Beth Pierce
Janet P. Caldwell * June 'Bugg' Barefield * Debbie M. Allen * Tony Henninger
Joe DaVerbal Minddancer * Robert Gibbons * Neetu Wali * Shareef Abdur-Rasheed
Kimberly Burnham * William S. Peters, Sr.

November Feature Poets
Jocelyn Mosman * Jackie Allen * James Moore * Neville Hiatt

THE YEAR OF THE POET
December 2014

Narcissus

The Poetry Posse
Jamie Bond
Gail Weston Shazor
Albert 'Infinite' Carrasco
Siddartha Beth Pierce
Janet P. Caldwell
June 'Bugg' Barefield
Debbie M. Allen
Tony Henninger
DaVerbal Minddancer
Robert Gibbons
Neetu Wali
Shareef Abdur-Rasheed
Kimberly Burnham
William S. Peters, Sr.

December Feature Poets
Katherine Wyatt* Writtenin... Santos Molino * Justin... ...ke

Now Available

www.innerchildpress.com/the-year-of-the-poet

THE YEAR OF THE POET II
January 2015

Garnet

The Poetry Posse

Jamie Bond
Gail Weston Shazor
Albert 'Infinite' Carrasco
Siddartha Beth Pierce
Janet P. Caldwell
Tony Henninger
Joe DaVerbal Minddancer
Robert Gibbons
Neetu Wali
Shareef Abdur - Rasheed
Kimberly Burnham
Ann White
Keith Alan Hamilton
Katherine Wyatt
Fahredin Shehu
Hülya N. Yılmaz
Teresa E. Gallion
Jackie Allen
William S. Peters, Sr.

January Feature Poets
Bismay Mohanti * Jen Walls * Eric Judah

THE YEAR OF THE POET II
February 2015

Amethyst

THE POETRY POSSE

Jamie Bond
Gail Weston Shazor
Albert 'Infinite' Carrasco
Siddartha Beth Pierce
Janet P. Caldwell
Tony Henninger
Joe DaVerbal Minddancer
Robert Gibbons
Neetu Wali
Shareef Abdur - Rasheed
Kimberly Burnham
Ann White
Keith Alan Hamilton
Katherine Wyatt
Fahredin Shehu
Hülya N. Yılmaz
Teresa E. Gallion
Jackie Allen
William S. Peters, Sr.

FEBRUARY FEATURE POETS
Iram Fatima * Bob McNeil * Kerstin Centervall

The Year of the Poet II
March 2015

Our Featured Poets
Heung Sook * Anthony Arnold * Alicia Poland

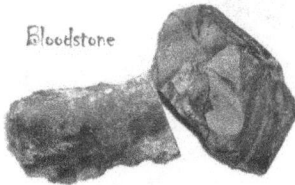

Bloodstone

The Poetry Posse 2015
Jamie Bond * Gail Weston Shazor * Albert 'Infinite' Carrasco
Siddartha Beth Pierce * Janet P. Caldwell * Tony Henninger
Joe DaVerbal Minddancer * Neetu Wali * Shareef Abdur – Rasheed
Kimberly Burnham * Ann White * Keith Alan Hamilton
Katherine Wyatt * Fahredin Shehu * Hülya N. Yılmaz
Teresa E. Gallion * Jackie Allen * William S. Peters, Sr

The Year of the Poet II
April 2015

Celebrating International Poetry Month

Our Featured Poets
Raja Williams * Dennis Ferado * Laure Charazac

Diamonds

The Poetry Posse 2015
Jamie Bond * Gail Weston Shazor * Albert 'Infinite' Carrasco
Siddartha Beth Pierce * Janet P. Caldwell * Tony Henninger
Joe DaVerbal Minddancer * Neetu Wali * Shareef Abdur – Rasheed
Kimberly Burnham * Ann White * Keith Alan Hamilton
Katherine Wyatt * Fahredin Shehu * Hülya N. Yılmaz
Teresa E. Gallion * Jackie Allen * William S. Peters, Sr

Now Available

www.innerchildpress.com/the-year-of-the-poet

The Year of the Poet II
May 2015

May's Featured Poets

Geri Algeri
Akin Mosi Chinney
Anna Jakubcza

Emeralds

The Poetry Posse 2015

Jamie Bond * Gail Weston Shazor * Albert 'Infinite' Carrasco
Siddartha Beth Pierce * Janet P. Caldwell * Tony Henninger
Joe DaVerbal Minddancer * Neetu Wali * Shareef Abdur – Rasheed
Kimberly Burnham * Ann White * Keith Alan Hamilton
Katherine Wyatt * Fahredin Shehu * Hülya N. Yılmaz
Teresa E. Gallion * Jackie Allen * William S. Peters, Sr.

The Year of the Poet II
June 2015

June's Featured Poets

Anahit Arustamyan * Yvette D. Murrell * Regina A. Walker

Pearl

The Poetry Posse 2015

Jamie Bond * Gail Weston Shazor * Albert 'Infinite' Carrasco
Siddartha Beth Pierce * Janet P. Caldwell * Tony Henninger
Joe DaVerbal Minddancer * Neetu Wali * Shareef Abdur – Rasheed
Kimberly Burnham * Ann White * Keith Alan Hamilton
Katherine Wyatt * Fahredin Shehu * Hülya N. Yılmaz
Teresa E. Gallion * Jackie Allen * William S. Peters, Sr.

The Year of the Poet II
July 2015

The Featured Poets for July 2015
Abhik Shome * Christina Neal * Robert Neal

Rubies

The Poetry Posse 2015

Jamie Bond * Gail Weston Shazor * Albert 'Infinite' Carrasco
Siddartha Beth Pierce * Janet P. Caldwell * Tony Henninger
Joe DaVerbal Minddancer * Neetu Wali * Shareef Abdur – Rasheed
Kimberly Burnham * Ann White * Keith Alan Hamilton
Katherine Wyatt * Fahredin Shehu * Hülya N. Yılmaz
Teresa E. Gallion * Jackie Allen * William S. Peters, Sr.

The Year of the Poet II
August 2015

Peridot

Featured Poets
Gayle Howell
Ann Chalasz
Christopher Schultz

The Poetry Posse 2015

Jamie Bond * Gail Weston Shazor * Albert 'Infinite' Carrasco
Siddartha Beth Pierce * Janet P. Caldwell * Tony Henninger
Joe DaVerbal Minddancer * Neetu Wali * Shareef Abdur – Rasheed
Kimberly Burnham * Ann White * Keith Alan Hamilton
Katherine Wyatt * Fahredin Shehu * Hülya N. Yılmaz
Teresa E. Gallion * Jackie Allen * William S. Peters, Sr.

Now Available

www.innerchildpress.com/the-year-of-the-poet

The Year of the Poet II
September 2015

Featured Poets
Alfreda Ghee * Lonneice Weeks Badley * Demetrios Trifiatis

Sapphires

The Poetry Posse 2015
Jamie Bond * Gail Weston Shazor * Albert 'Infinite' Carrasco
Siddartha Beth Pierce * Janet P. Caldwell * Tony Henninger
Joe DaVerbal Minddancer * Neetu Wali * Shareef Abdur – Rasheed
Kimberly Burnham * Ann White * Keith Alan Hamilton
Katherine Wyatt * Fahredin Shehu * Hülya N. Yılmaz
Teresa E. Gallion * Jackie Allen * William S. Peters, Sr.

The Year of the Poet II
October 2015

Featured Poets
Monte Smith * Laura J. Wolfe * William Washington

Opal

The Poetry Posse 2015
Jamie Bond * Gail Weston Shazor * Albert 'Infinite' Carrasco
Siddartha Beth Pierce * Janet P. Caldwell * Tony Henninger
Joe DaVerbal Minddancer * Neetu Wali * Shareef Abdur – Rasheed
Kimberly Burnham * Ann White * Keith Alan Hamilton
Katherine Wyatt * Fahredin Shehu * Hülya N. Yılmaz
Teresa E. Gallion * Jackie Allen * William S. Peters, Sr.

The Year of the Poet II
November 2015

Featured Poets
Alan W. Jankowski
Itishree Mohanty
James Moore

Topaz

The Poetry Posse 2015
Jamie Bond * Gail Weston Shazor * Albert 'Infinite' Carrasco
Siddartha Beth Pierce * Janet P. Caldwell * Tony Henninger
Joe DaVerbal Minddancer * Neetu Wali * Shareef Abdur – Rasheed
Kimberly Burnham * Ann White * Keith Alan Hamilton
Katherine Wyatt * Fahredin Shehu * Hülya N. Yılmaz
Teresa E. Gallion * Jackie Allen * William S. Peters, Sr.

The Year of the Poet II
December 2015

Featured Poets
Kerione Bryan * Michelle Joan Barulich * Neville Hiatt

Turquoise

The Poetry Posse 2015
Jamie Bond * Gail Weston Shazor * Albert 'Infinite' Carrasco
Siddartha Beth Pierce * Janet P. Caldwell * Tony Henninger
Joe DaVerbal Minddancer * Neetu Wali * Shareef Abdur – Rasheed
Kimberly Burnham * Ann White * Keith Alan Hamilton
Katherine Wyatt * Fahredin Shehu * Hülya N. Yılmaz
Teresa E. Gallion * Jackie Allen * William S. Peters, Sr.

Now Available

www.innerchildpress.com/the-year-of-the-poet

The Year of the Poet III
January 2016

Featured Poets
Lana Joseph * Atom Cyrus Rush * Christena Williams

Dark-eyed Junco

The Poetry Posse 2016

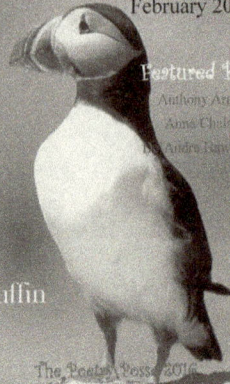

The Year of the Poet III
February 2016

Featured Poets
Anthony Arnold
Anna Chalasz
De Andre Rawstorne

Puffin

The Poetry Posse 2016

The Year of the Poet
March 2016

Featured Poets
Jeton Kelmendi   Nizar Sartawi   Sami Muhanna

Robin

The Poetry Posse 2016

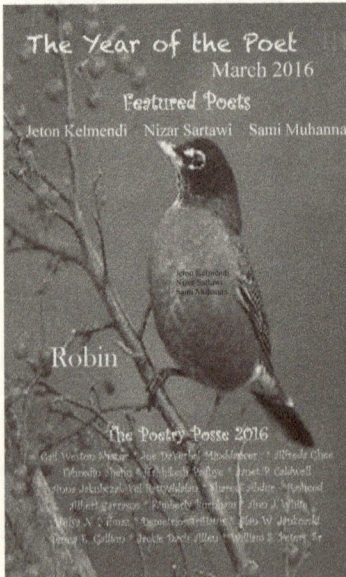

The Year of the Poet III

Featured Poets

Ali Abdolrezaei

Anna Chalasz

Agim Vinca

Ceri Naz

Black Capped Chickadee

The Poetry Posse 2016

celebrating international poetry month

Now Available

www.innerchildpress.com/the-year-of-the-poet

The Year of the Poet III
September 2016

Featured Poets

Simone Weber
Abhijit Sen
Eunice Barbara C. Novio

Long Billed Curle

The Poetry Posse 2016

The Year of the Poet III
October 2016

Featured Poets

Lewis Joseph
Krishnamurthy
James Moore

Barn Owl

The Poetry Posse 2016

The Year of the Poet III
November 2016

Featured Poets

Rosemary Burns
Robin Ouzman Hislop
Lonneice Weeks-Badley

Northern Cardinal

The Poetry Posse 2016

Gail Weston Shazor * Carolina Nazzaro * Jen Walls
Nizar Sartawi * Janet P. Caldwell * Alfredo Chea
Joe DaVerbal Minddancer * Shareef Abdur - Rasheed
Albert Carrasco * Kimberly Burnham * Elizabeth Castillo
Hülya N. Yılmaz * Demetrios Trifiatis * Alan W. Jankowski
Teresa E. Gallion * Jackie Davis Allen * William S. Peters, Sr.

The Year of the Poet III
December 2016

Featured Poets

Samíh Masoud
Mountassir Aziz Bien
Abdulkadir Musa

Rough Legged Hawk

The Poetry Posse 2016

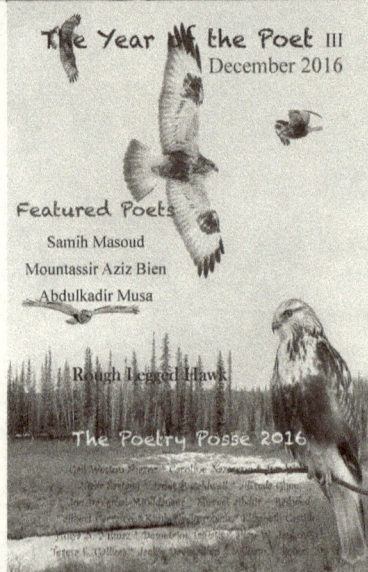

Now Available

www.innerchildpress.com/the-year-of-the-poet

The Year of the Poet IV
January 2017

Featured Poets
Jen Walls
Natalie Shields
Hani Fatima 'Ashi'

Quaking Aspen

The Poetry Posse 2017

Gail Weston Shazor * Caroline Nazareno * Hulya Yilmaz
Nizar Sartawi * Anne Jakubczak Val Batty Alsdorf * Jen Walls
Joe DaVerbal Minddancer * Shareef Abdur – Rasheed
Albert Carrasco * Kimberly Burnham * Elizabeth Castillo
Hulya N. Yilmaz * Faleeha Hassan * Alan W. Jankowski
Teresa E. Gallion * Jackie Davis Allen * William S. Peters, Sr.

The Year of the Poet IV
February 2017

Featured Poets
Lin Ross
Soukaina Fathi
Anwer Ghani

Witch Hazel

The Poetry Posse 2017

Gail Weston Shazor * Caroline Nazareno * Hulya Yilmaz
Nizar Sartawi * Anne Jakubczak Val Batty Alsdorf * Jen Walls
Joe DaVerbal Minddancer * Shareef Abdur – Rasheed
Albert Carrasco * Kimberly Burnham * Elizabeth Castillo
Hulya N. Yilmaz * Faleeha Hassan * Alan W. Jankowski
Teresa E. Gallion * Jackie Davis Allen * William S. Peters, Sr.

The Year of the Poet IV
March 2017

Featured Poets
Tremell Stevens
Francisca Ricinski
Jamil Abu Shaih

The Eastern Redbud

The Poetry Posse 2017

Gail Weston Shazor * Caroline Nazareno * Hulya Yilmaz
Teresa E. Gallion * Anne Jakubczak Val Batty Alsdorf
Joe DaVerbal Minddancer * Shareef Abdur – Rasheed
Albert Carrasco * Kimberly Burnham * Elizabeth Castillo
Hulya N. Yilmaz * Faleeha Hassan * Jackie Davis Allen
Jen Walls * Nizar Sartawi * * William S. Peters, Sr.

The Year of the Poet IV
April 2017

Featured Poets
Dr. Rachida Bazman
Neptune Barman
Masood Khalaf

The Blossoming Cherry

The Poetry Posse 2017

Gail Weston Shazor * Caroline Nazareno * Hulya Yilmaz
Teresa E. Gallion * Anne Jakubczak Val Batty Alsdorf
Joe DaVerbal Minddancer * Shareef Abdur – Rasheed
Albert Carrasco * Kimberly Burnham * Elizabeth Castillo
Hulya N. Yilmaz * Faleeha Hassan * Jackie Davis Allen
Jen Walls * Nizar Sartawi * * William S. Peters, Sr.

Now Available

www.innerchildpress.com/the-year-of-the-poet

The Year of the Poet IV
May 2017

The Flowering Dogwood Tree

Featured Poets

Kallisa Powell

Alicja Maria Kuberska

Fethi Sassi

The Poetry Posse 2017

Gail Weston Shazor * Caroline Nazareno * Panay Mohanty
Teresa E. Gallion * Anna Jakubczak Vel Ratty Adalan
Joe DaVerbal Minddancer * Shareef Abdur – Rasheed
Albert Carrasco * Kimberly Burnham * Elizabeth Castillo
Hülya N. Yılmaz * Eliesha Hayes * Jackie Davis Allen
Jen Walls * Nizar Sartawi * * William S. Peters, Sr.

The Year of the Poet IV
June 2017

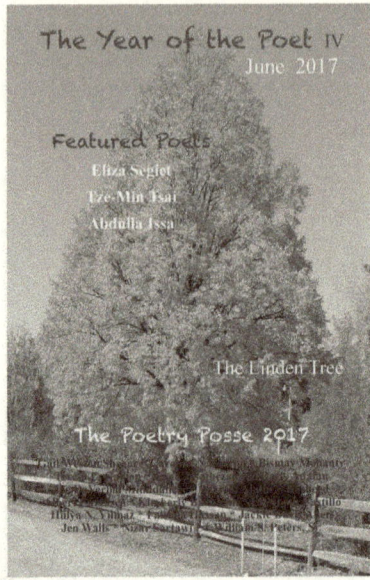

Featured Poets

Eliza Segiet

Tze-Min Tsai

Abdulla Issa

The Linden Tree

The Poetry Posse 2017

Gail Weston Shazor * Caroline Nazareno * Panay Mohanty
Teresa E. Gallion * Anna Jakubczak Vel Ratty Adalan
Joe DaVerbal Minddancer * Shareef Abdur – Rasheed
Albert Carrasco * Kimberly Burnham * Elizabeth Castillo
Hülya N. Yılmaz * Eliesha Hayes * Jackie Davis Allen
Jen Walls * Nizar Sartawi * * William S. Peters, Sr.

The Year of the Poet IV
July 2017

Featured Poets

Anca Mihaela Bruma

Ibaa Ismail

Zvonko Taneski

The Oak Moon

The Poetry Posse 2017

Gail Weston Shazor * Caroline Nazareno * Panay Mohanty
Teresa E. Gallion * Anna Jakubczak Vel Ratty Adalan
Joe DaVerbal Minddancer * Shareef Abdur – Rasheed
Albert Carrasco * Kimberly Burnham * Elizabeth Castillo
Hülya N. Yılmaz * Eliesha Hayes * Jackie Davis Allen
Jen Walls * Nizar Sartawi * * William S. Peters, Sr.

The Year of the Poet IV
August 2017

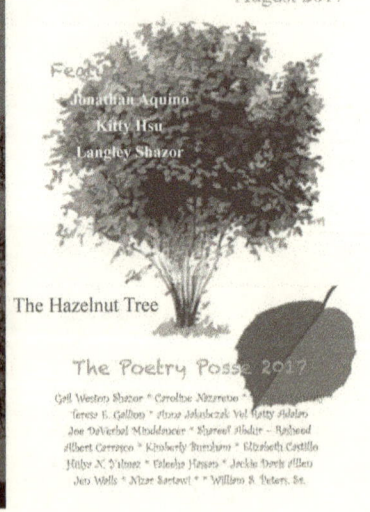

Featured Poets

Jonathan Aquino

Kitty Hsu

Langley Shazor

The Hazelnut Tree

The Poetry Posse 2017

Gail Weston Shazor * Caroline Nazareno * Panay Mohanty
Teresa E. Gallion * Anna Jakubczak Vel Ratty Adalan
Joe DaVerbal Minddancer * Shareef Abdur – Rasheed
Albert Carrasco * Kimberly Burnham * Elizabeth Castillo
Hülya N. Yılmaz * Eliesha Hayes * Jackie Davis Allen
Jen Walls * Nizar Sartawi * * William S. Peters, Sr.

Now Available

www.innerchildpress.com/the-year-of-the-poet

The Year of the Poet IV
September 2017

Featured Poets

Martina Reisz Newber...

Ameer Nassir

Christine Fulco Nea...

Robert Neal

The Elm Tree

The Poetry Posse 2017

Gail Weston Shazor * Caroline Nazareno * Bismay Mohanty
Teresa E. Gallion * Anna Jakubczak Vel Ratty Adalan
Joe DaVerbal Minddancer * Shareef Abdur – Rasheed
Albert Carrasco * Kimberly Burnham * Elizabeth Castillo
Hülya N. Yılmaz * Faleeha Hassan * Jackie Davis Allen
Jen Walls * Nizar Sartawi * * William S. Peters, Sr.

The Year of the Poet IV
October 2017

Featured Poets

Ahmed Abu Saleem

Nedal Al-Qaeim

Sadeddin Shahin

The Black Walnut Tree

The Poetry Posse 2017

Gail Weston Shazor * Caroline Nazareno * Bismay Mohanty
Teresa E. Gallion * Anna Jakubczak Vel Ratty Adalan
Joe DaVerbal Minddancer * Shareef Abdur – Rasheed
Albert Carrasco * Kimberly Burnham * Elizabeth Castillo
Hülya N. Yılmaz * Faleeha Hassan * Jackie Davis Allen
Jen Walls * Nizar Sartawi * * William S. Peters, Sr.

The Year of the Poet IV
November 2017

Featured Poets

Kay Peters

Alfreda D. Ghee

Gabriella Garofalo

Rosemary Cappello

The Tree of Life

The Poetry Posse 2017

Gail Weston Shazor * Caroline Nazareno * Bismay Mohanty
Teresa E. Gallion * Anna Jakubczak Vel Ratty Adalan
Joe DaVerbal Minddancer * Shareef Abdur – Rasheed
Albert Carrasco * Kimberly Burnham * Elizabeth Castillo
Hülya N. Yılmaz * Faleeha Hassan * Jackie Davis Allen
Jen Walls * Nizar Sartawi * William S. Peters, Sr.

The Year of the Poet IV
December 2017

Featured Poets

Justice Clarke

Mariel M. Pabroa

Kiley Brown

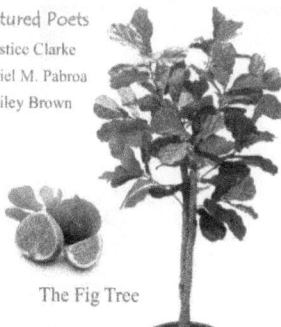

The Fig Tree

The Poetry Posse 2017

Gail Weston Shazor * Caroline Nazareno * Bismay Mohanty
Teresa E. Gallion * Anna Jakubczak Vel Ratty Adalan
Joe DaVerbal Minddancer * Shareef Abdur – Rasheed
Albert Carrasco * Kimberly Burnham * Elizabeth Castillo
Hülya N. Yılmaz * Faleeha Hassan * Jackie Davis Allen
Jen Walls * Nizar Sartawi * William S. Peters, Sr.

Now Available

www.innerchildpress.com/the-year-of-the-poet

The Year of the Poet V
January 2018
Featured Poets
Iyad Shamasnah
Yasmeen Hamzeh
Ali Abdolrezaei

Aksum

The Poetry Posse 2018
Gail Weston Shazor * Caroline Nazareno * Tezmin Ition Tsai
Hülya N. Yılmaz * Faleeha Hassan * Jackie Davis Allen
Teresa E. Gallion * Anna Jakubczak Vel Ratty Adalan
Alicja Maria Kuberska * Shareef Abdur – Rasheed
Kimberly Burnham * Elizabeth Castillo
Nizar Sartawi * William S. Peters, Sr.

The Year of the Poet V
February 2018

Sabean

Featured Poets
Muhammad Azram
Anna Szawrocka
Abhilipsa Kuanar
Aanika Aery

The Poetry Posse 2018
Gail Weston Shazor * Caroline Nazareno * Tezmin Ition Tsai
Hülya N. Yılmaz * Faleeha Hassan * Jackie Davis Allen
Teresa E. Gallion * Anna Jakubczak Vel Ratty Adalan
Alicja Maria Kuberska * Shareef Abdur – Rasheed
Kimberly Burnham * Elizabeth Castillo
Nizar Sartawi * William S. Peters, Sr.

The Year of the Poet V
March 2018

Featured Poets
Iram Fatima 'Aabi'
Cassandra Swan
Jaleel Khazaal
Shazia Zaman

Mexico
Cuba
Dominican
Republic
Belize
Haiti
Puerto Rico
Guatemala
Honduras
Jamaica
El Salvador
Nicaragua
Costa Rica
Panama
Caribbean
&
Middle America
Colombia

The Poetry Posse 2018
Gail Weston Shazor * Nizar Sartawi * Hülya N. Yılmaz
Jackie Davis Allen * Caroline 'Ceri' Nazareno
Alicja Maria Kuberska * Teresa E. Gallion
Faleeha Hassan * Shareef Abdur – Rasheed
Kimberly Burnham * Elizabeth Castillo
Tezmin Ition Tsai * William S. Peters, Sr.

The Year of the Poet V
April 2018

Featured Poets

The Nez Perce

The Poetry Posse 2018

Now Available

www.innerchildpress.com/the-year-of-the-poet

190

The Year of the Poet V
May 2018

Featured Poets
Zaldy Carreon de Leon Jr.
Sylwia K. Malinowska
Lindita Ahmeti
Ofelia Prodan
The Sumerians

The Poetry Posse 2018
Gail Weston Shazor * Nizar Sartawi * Hülya N. Yılmaz
Jackie Davis Allen * Caroline 'Ceri' Nazareno
Alicja Maria Kuberska * Teresa E. Gallion
Kimberly Burnham * Shareef Abdur – Rasheed
Faleeha Hassan * Elizabeth Castillo * Swapna Behera
Tezmin Ition Tsai * William S. Peters, Sr.

The Year of the Poet V
June 2018

Featured Poets
Bilall Maliqi * Daim Miftari * Gojko Božović * Sofija Živković

The Paleo Indians

The Poetry Posse 2018
Gail Weston Shazor * Nizar Sartawi * Hülya N. Yılmaz
Jackie Davis Allen * Caroline 'Ceri' Nazareno
Alicja Maria Kuberska * Teresa E. Gallion
Kimberly Burnham * Shareef Abdur – Rasheed
Faleeha Hassan * Elizabeth Castillo * Swapna Behera
Tezmin Ition Tsai * William S. Peters, Sr.

The Year of the Poet V
July 2018

Featured Poets
Padmaja Iyengar-Paddy
Muhammad Ikbal Harb
Eliza Segiet
Tom Higgins

Oceania

The Poetry Posse 2018
Gail Weston Shazor * Nizar Sartawi * Hülya N. Yılmaz
Jackie Davis Allen * Caroline 'Ceri' Nazareno
Alicja Maria Kuberska * Teresa E. Gallion
Kimberly Burnham * Shareef Abdur – Rasheed
Faleeha Hassan * Elizabeth Castillo * Swapna Behera
Tezmin Ition Tsai * William S. Peters, Sr.

The Year of the Poet V
August 2018

Featured Poets
Hussein Habasch * Mircea Dan Duta * Naida Mujkić * Swagat Das

The Lapita

The Poetry Posse 2018
Gail Weston Shazor * Nizar Sartawi * Hülya N. Yılmaz
Jackie Davis Allen * Caroline 'Ceri' Nazareno
Alicja Maria Kuberska * Teresa E. Gallion
Kimberly Burnham * Shareef Abdur – Rasheed
Ashok K. Bhargava* Elizabeth Castillo * Swapna Behaera
Tezmin Ition Tsai * William S. Peters, Sr.

Now Available

www.innerchildpress.com/the-year-of-the-poet

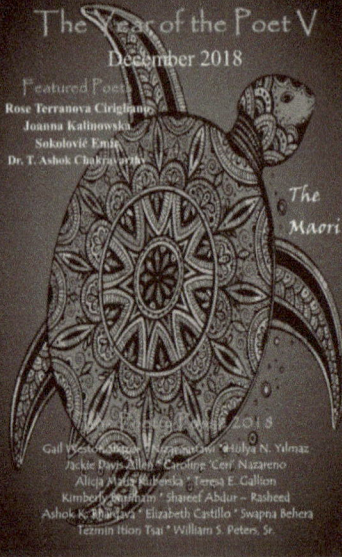

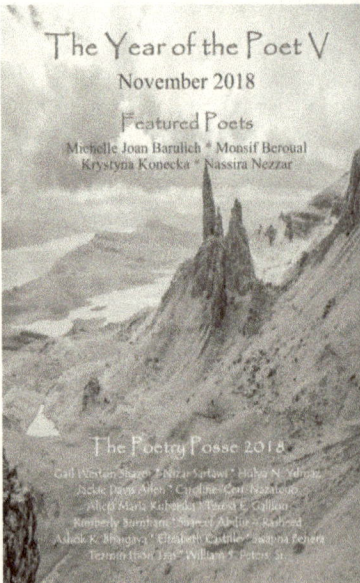

192

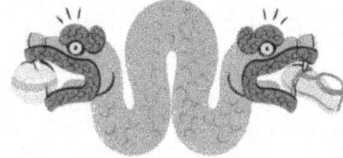

and there is much, much more !

visit . . .

www.innerchildpress.com/antho
logies-sales-special.php

Also check out our Authors and
all the wonderful Books
Available at :

www.innerchildpress.com/autho
rs-pages

INNER CHILD PRESS

WORLD HEALING WORLD PEACE

2018

A Poetry Anthology for Humanity

Now Available

www.worldhealingworldpeacepoetry.com

Now Available

196

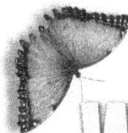

World Healing
World Peace

support

www.worldhealingworldpeacepoetry.com

World Healing World Peace Poetry

i am a believer!

World Healing
World Peace
2018

Now Available

www.worldhealingworldpeacepoetry.com

Inner Child Press International

'building bridges of cultural understanding'

Meet the Board of Directors

William S. Peters, Sr.
Chair Person
Founder
Inner Child Enterprises
Inner Child Press

Hülya N Yılmaz
Director
Editing Services
Co-Chair Person

Fahredin B. Shehu
Director
Cultural Affairs

Elizabeth E. Castillo
Director
Recording Secretary

De'Andre Hawthorne
Director
Performance Poetry

Gail Weston Shazor
Director
Anthologies

Kimberly Burnham
Director
Cultural Ambassador
Pacific Northwest
USA

Ashok K. Bhargava
Director
WINAwards

Deborah Smart
Director
Publicity
Marketing

www.innerchildpress.com

Inner Child Press International

'building bridges of cultural understanding'

Meet our Cultural Ambassadors

Fahredin Shehu
Director of Cultural

Faleha Hassan
Iraq ~ USA

Elizabeth E. Castillo
Philippines

Antoinette Coleman
Chicago
Midwest USA

Ananda Nepali
Nepal ~ Pune
Northern India

Kimberly Burnham
Pacific Northwest
USA

Alicja Kuberska
Poland
Eastern Europe

Swapna Behera
India
Southeast Asia

Kolade O. Freedom
Nigeria
West Africa

Monsif Beroual
Morocco
Northern Afric

Ashok K. Bhargava
Canada

Tzemin Ition Tsai
Republic of China
Greater China

Alicia M. Ramirez
Mexico
Central America

Christena AV Williams
Jamaica
Caribbean

Louise Hudon
Eastern Canada

Aziz Mountassir
Morocco
Northern Africa

Shareef Abdur-Rasheed
Southeastern USA

Laure Charazac
France
Western Europe

Mohammad Ikbal Harb
Lebanon
Middle East

Mohamed Abdel Aziz Shmeis
Egypt
Middle East

Hilary Mainga
Kenya
Eastern Africa

Josephus R. Johnson
Liberia

www.innerchildpress.com

200

This Anthological Publication
is underwritten solely by

Inner Child Press

Inner Child Press is a Publishing Company Founded and Operated by Writers. Our personal publishing experiences provides us an intimate understanding of the sometimes daunting challenges Writers, New and Seasoned may face in the Business of Publishing and Marketing their Creative "Written Work".

For more Information

Inner Child Press

www.innerchildpress.com

Inner Child Press International

'building bridges of cultural understanding'
202 Wiltree Court, State College, Pennsylvania 16801

www.innerchildpress.com

~ fini ~

www.ingramcontent.com/pod-product-compliance
Lightning Source LLC
LaVergne TN
LVHW011154080426
835508LV00007B/390